THE LONDON
BENDY BUS

PEN & SWORD
TRANSPORT

MATTHEW WHARMBY

CONTENTS

DEDICATION

To Owen and Fred, my nephews.

Published in 2016 by Pen & Sword Transport
an imprint of
Pen & Sword Books Ltd
47 Church Street, Barnsley, South Yorkshire, S70 2AS

Copyright © Matthew Wharmby, 2016

ISBN 978 1 78383 172 2

Typeset by Matthew Wharmby

Printed and bound in India by Replika Press Pvt. Ltd.

Pen & Sword Books Ltd incorporates the imprints of Pen & Sword Archaeology, Atlas, Aviation, Battleground, Discovery, Family History, History, Maritime, Military, Naval, Politics, Railways, Select, Transport, True Crime, and Fiction, Frontline Books, Leo Cooper, Praetorian Press, Seaforth Publishing and Wharncliffe.

For a complete list of Pen & Sword titles please contact
PEN & SWORD BOOKS LIMITED
47 Church Street, Barnsley, South Yorkshire, S70 2AS, England
E-mail: enquiries@pen-and-sword.co.uk
Website: www.pen-and-sword.co.uk

THE BUS WE HATED

Between 2002 and 2006 six of London's bus companies put into service 390 articulated 'bendy' buses on twelve routes on behalf of Transport for London. During what turned out to be a foreshortened nine years in service, the Mercedes-Benz Citaro G buses familiar on the continent and worldwide earned an unenviable reputation in London; according to who you read and who you believed, they caught fire at the drop of a hat, they maimed cyclists, they drained revenue from the system due to their susceptibility to fare evasion, they transported already long-suffering passengers in standing crush loads like cattle and they contributed to the extinction of the Routemaster from frontline service. In short, the bus we hated.

I know I didn't care for them – there's no doubt about that. Irrational as it sounds, they just weren't 'British' – as vehicles or as cultural phenomena. They seemed to represent an imperative that was as far from British as it's possible to be; communal, disdainful of tradition and pandering to the unattractive habit of the modern British to do themselves down at every turn. If no 'European' cities strove to be like London, for example, why were those who ran London seemingly obsessed with subsuming its independence and character into an amorphous Europe? Therefore, the challenge of this book is to set aside ingrained prejudices about the suitability, culturally, aesthetically or otherwise, of these bendy buses, and attempt to give their supporters as well as their detractors the benefit of the doubt. Without quite rehabilitating them, this book attempts to set the vehicles in their proper context, and to be as fair as possible towards a mode of transport which was unwelcome in London and which is, at least until tastes change again, behind us.

Matthew Wharmby
Walton-on-Thames, July 2015

Below: **The lifespan of London's bendy buses coincided with the reintroduction of all-over advertisements using improved methods of printing and vinyl application. A pair of Stagecoach East London artics based on the 25 served as recruitment devices for the University of East London, one in orange and the other, 23033 (LX03 HEJ) in blue. During April 2005 it is seen against the elegant backdrop of the Prudential building in High Holborn.** *Haydn Davies*

CHAPTER ONE

DEMONSTRATORS

Below: **Its unfortunate dependence upon British Leyland in the 1970s and no small amount of prideful protectionism caused London Transport to neglect comparable Continental chassis which were eating into hitherto surefire worldwide markets for British chassis. Therefore it had no experience of the Mercedes-Benz O.405 series and its articulated O.405G offshoot. Trans Island Bus Service (TIBS) of Singapore introduced a number of Hispano-bodied O.405Gs in 1996/97, one of which, TIB 868X, is at Choa Chu Kang on 16 June 1999. Singapore Bus Service (SBS) were already operating O.305s (double-deck at that!) and O.405s.** *Author*

For all London's supposed reputation as an impossible place to run buses either efficiently or profitably, the opposite is probably true, and all it has ever taken is a simple appreciation of the availability of space. Almost as soon as George Shillibeer hitched up his horses, the passengers of his early fixed routes would clamber onto the roof of the horse buses once they saw that space had run out in the main body of the vehicle. Not long after that, operators added seats to the roof and a staircase to get the passengers there, creating the first double-deck bus. As with buildings, the sheer lack of space to expand outwards in London made expanding upwards the logical and sensible option. Seating, comfortable or otherwise, has always been the London bus passenger's over-riding concern, competing even with

price and frequency, and the lack of it, when it is encountered, deeply resented; somehow, it is almost personal an insult, as if the operator can't be bothered to make what is seen as the minimum effort in return for the price the passenger is compelled to pay. While not an entitlement mentality as such, that unwritten and invisible contract between the public and the public servant has always been a delicate line to walk, and operators are advised to think about it with the same attention they rightfully give to efficiency and profit.

Despite the spread of the articulated bus to the Continent and worldwide, London Transport remained blissfully ignorant of its existence, for one reason or another having enough problems adapting its traditional bus model to something more modern in the shape of front-entrance, rear-entrance

Left: **And when they tried Continental-style bus transport in its unadulterated sense in London, it both worked like a charm (with the Red Arrows) and flopped horribly (everywhere else). Even within one city the needs of the centre versus those of the suburbs proved as disparate as could be. On 5 May 1981, with three weeks left to go in service, MBA 530 (VLW 530G) is seen under the canopy at Victoria on the 500; certainly no points off for the attractive Merlins, but it was under the skin that the problems arose. Even so, twelve years were wrung out of the Red Arrow MBAs.** *R. C. Riley*

Left: **The Leyland National, while controversial at the time for its enforced deletion of a host of other popular chassis, settled down to be a reliable and versatile steed without a great deal of glamour to get in the way of the simple need to shift short-hop passengers from A to B. The National 2 was a development that repositioned the radiator to the front for a more brute appearance. Again, the very utmost was got out of these vehicles, the Greenway project of 1993 buying what became the GLS class another eight years to inch them into two decades' service, and depicted coming to the end of that term on 23 April 2002 is GLS 492 (GUW 492W).** *Matthew Wharmby*

Right: **In February 1978 LT took a look at the first MAN SG192 built with a view to tempting British lawmakers to amend the legislation prohibiting articulated buses from stage service. There followed attachment to a handful of operators, most notably City of Oxford, which put it to use on Park & Ride work. On 24 June 1979 it is taking passengers from Uxbridge to Showbus at Hillingdon. Its Swiss (Zürich) registration 684 Z 7766 would be replaced by CLM 346T before the bus went off to South Yorkshire PTE, which did take artics, albeit Leyland-DAB examples; it was later used by Midland Red and lasted until 1987.** *Clive A. Brown*

Above right and right: **Amid the unedifying spectacle of company homogenisation seen in the 1970s, there were a few organisations brave (or mad) enough to gamble on untried chassis and experimental forms of transport. South Yorkshire PTE, already famous (or notorious) for its low-fares policy, took a punt on articulated buses in 1985 with an order for thirteen Leyland-DAB vehicles, having already tried out four. Seven years later, as the London Buses subsidiaries were finding their own feet in terms of orders of their own, Selkent took one of them on hire, and here is 2001 (C101 HDT) operating on a shortworking of the 180, which had to be thus because the route's southern terminus at that time was Hither Green Station, where artics (and the tri-axle Hong Kong Citybus Leyland Olympian evaluated at the same time) would not fit.** *Both: Bill Young*

OMO vehicles. LT looked over a Danish-built Leyland-DAB in July 1977 and in February 1978 inspected a MAN SG192 demonstrator and a Volvo/Van Hool counterpart at Chiswick works, with an eye to possible Red Arrow use if legislation prohibiting the use of artics was relaxed. However, it was as the centre crumbled that Selkent, one of the eleven pre-privatisation London Buses Ltd subsidiaries carved out in 1989, thought it would have a try at evaluating an existing UK model. There was no suggestion of bidding for a contract using such vehicles, which had only been permitted for British stage operation since 1980.

From 6 April 1992 Selkent thus took on loan C101 HDT, otherwise known as South Yorkshire 2001, a Leyland-DAB articulated bus from a batch of thirteen new in 1985 and operated by SYT on route 500 (City Centre–Moorfoot). It had already been on loan to CIE in Dublin. The vehicle was 17.35m long with three doors, seating 61 plus another 73 standing, and already its limitations became clear in that the Hither Green terminus of Plumstead's route 180, where it was going to operate, was not suitable; this stand had only been instituted the previous year and indeed the former terminus at Catford Garage was brought back into use for the occasion. It also had to miss out some of the trickier roads in Woolwich town centre. The working was

thus identified internally as 180A but this was not displayed on the bus due to it having only three-track number blinds. Operating between 6 April and 2 May, with a side trip to 1992's edition of the Cobham Bus Rally held at Apps Court in Walton-on-Thames, the artic garnered favourable comment from passengers, who particularly appreciated its extra floor space.

A little later, Capital Citybus, one of the new independent companies which (as Ensignbus) had been particularly lucky in winning extensive tendered work sufficient to prompt an international buyout, bid for the Red Arrow routes during 1994 by acquiring former British Airways airside Leyland-DAB RLN 233W and painting it in their current livery of yellow with two red stripes and full blinds, just to see what such operation might look like. It made its debut in yellow at the North Weald rally on 26 June 1994. This bus originally had four doors, one set being on the offside, but this was removed to offer a capacity of AB59D+62. Three more from the batch of seven were acquired, RLN 234W, RLN 238W and another, in the hope of perhaps putting them on school route 550, but this did not come to fruition. Nor did Capital Citybus win the Red Arrows, as it turned out, the routes remaining with London General, but the articulated bus concept, while dormant, was not forgotten.

CHAPTER TWO

THE 207 TRIALS

Below: **Volvo's articulated chassis of the time was the B10LA, and four of those new to First in Glasgow since 1999 were borrowed by Centrewest for trials. The physical nature of the 207 – long and straight – seemed to lend itself to the use of artics, but failed to take into account passengers' wish to have a seat. Numbered AV 8 (V608 GGB) for the duration, this Barbie-liveried B10LA passes through West Ealing in April 2002.** *Haydn Davies*

On Monday 15 October 2001 First Uxbridge Buses put into service six artics on the 207, which was at that time still a powerful trunk route, although operating in two overlapping sections with express route 607 serving both widely-spread terminals on a limited-stop basis. Thoughts of turning this former tram and trolleybus corridor into a modern tram line known as West London Transit were swirling around TfL's higher echelons, having seen the success of Croydon Tramlink, and traffic conditions along the Uxbridge Road, beset by pinch points as the 207 moved in and out of built-up areas like Southall and Ealing, were growing worse rather than better. The next best solution to trams was artics, it was felt, and their success or failure over the part of the 207 selected would furnish useful information for the spreading of the mode.

The six bendies comprised two Wrightbus Eclipse Fusion-bodied Volvo B7LAs, AVs 1 and 2 (Y151, 152 ROT) seconded from First Southampton, and four of the older combination of Wright Fusion-bodied Volvo B10LA, brought down from First Glasgow

as AV 6-8 and 10 (V606-608, 610 GGB). All retained FirstGroup 'Barbie' livery except AV 1, which received the current First London red with white and grey willow leaf device. All dual-doored, the B7LAs seated 56 and the B10LAs 55. They operated an additional schedule to the usual Uxbridge and Acton Tram Depot allocations, and since neither of these garages could accommodate them, were based at Greenford (G), the former Royal Mail depot with plenty of unencumbered outdoor space to turn around in. This was the first

Above: **Wright's Eclipse bodies received different sub-names according to the chassis they rode atop; thus on articulated Volvo chassis it was the Eclipse Fusion. AV 2 is seen west of Ealing in May 2002.**
Haydn Davies

instance of garaging problems which were to dictate so much which premises would be able to operate bendies, though it wasn't so much the turning circle of the things but the acreage taken up when straightened out.

Although the trials were meant to last only three or four months, the artics were retained into 2002 pending the delivery of ten more Tridents to furnish a whopping ten-bus PVR increase on the 207 from 27 April. As it happened, appearances of the B10LAs and B7LAs dwindled in practice towards the end of the trials, with none at all seen on some days.

Above: **For the 207 trials one of the pair of B7LA artics was repainted in the current First London livery of red with white and yellow stripes curling down into the 'willow leaf' style. AV 1 (Y151 ROT) heads east towards Ealing in November 2001.** *Haydn Davies*

Left: **AV 1 (Y151 ROT) passes the entrance to Ealing Hospital during April 2002. While the concealed wheel wells were futuristic-looking, they were a nightmare to clean and were not taken up on this design or any subsequent.** *Haydn Davies*

Below: **AV 1 (Y151 ROT) also made an appearance at Cobham for 2002, standing out as something different some time before bendies became** *persona non grata* **at rallies.** *Author*

CHAPTER THREE

2002

Introduced on 7 September 1968 as part of the massive Reshaping changes, the 507 was the only Red Arrow route to stay the course; its simple remit taking civil servants and other office types to and from a choice of railheads at Victoria and Waterloo couldn't be challenged, and indeed over the years the competing stage services fell back until the 507 was by the end of the century the only way to travel between Waterloo and Victoria.

Inaugurated from Victoria garage with MBAs, the route kept this type for over a decade; like the bendies that would follow two generations of buses later, the Merlins were ideally suited to Red Arrow work. SMSs filtered in as support towards the end of the 1970s and were withdrawn together with the MBAs on 2 July 1981, when new Leyland National 2s took over. These vehicles, occupying the highest stock numbers of the LS class, would have a long career, helped out by their extensive rebuild in 1993 into National Greenways (GLSs). From 28 October 1990 they were working from Waterloo (RA), the former bus station rebuilt with fuel tanks as an ideally situated open-field garage in the heart of London. An attempt to move the route to Victoria's minibus-operating basement at the same time so that Waterloo would not operate at weekends (and thereby placate the local residents upset at vehicle noise and fumes) did not last, and the 507 settled down to Monday to Friday operation.

The GLSs spanned the privatisation of London Buses Ltd in the autumn of 1994, which brought London General under its management. In 1996 this company was sold to the Go-Ahead Group and federated with London Central, its existing ex-LBL acquisition. The core Red Arrow routes settled down after a long period of tinkering to determine just where the peak passenger flows were, which, unfortunately, was generally not along Oxford Street or in the West End as a whole. Where the passengers wanted to go was to and from the major railheads to their workplaces in the City or the large government facilities around Victoria, so by the end of the century all other termini ever served by the Red Arrows, from Marylebone to Pall Mall, had been abandoned.

By the turn of the century the GLSs were time-expired by anyone's reckoning, but the tender award which returned the routes to London General under Tranche 93 was only to be for 15 months pending scrutiny of travel patterns following the opening of the Jubilee Line extension. That period, which bought the GLSs enough time to get them to their 20th anniversary on aggregate, saw the 505 taken off with effect from 19 August 2000. It had replaced normal buses on the Old Street–Waterloo corridor (the 5 and 55) and was itself replaced by a normal bus (an extension of the 243). When that period was up the routes were tendered again under Tranche 125 in January 2001, and anyone who thought they had a chance would be obliged to bid with new vehicles.

London General had added some spice to its bid by specifying articulated buses and this was what secured it the contract, a standard five-year term awarded in July but not to take effect until the vehicles had been delivered. To this end, 31 Mercedes-Benz O.530G Citaros were ordered in October for spring 2002 delivery, by which time it was hoped that the way people were going to be expected to board these three-doored vehicles would be firmed up. The rollout date of a long-promised smartcard system would be key to all this, but for the moment, with three doors on each artic, what was the

Left: **At least when specifying chassis for the artic routes there was a basis to work from already in place; wary of getting burned once again by mass ordering untried chassis yet without the time or patience really to evaluate anything properly, TfL took fixed Citaros for the RV1, which at one point was envisaged as a testbed for battery-operated vehicles or even modern trolleybuses. Citaros were subsequently felt modern enough and twelve were ordered with the RV1's award to First Capital. On 27 August 2002 Hackney's EC 2009 (LT02 NUH) calls at Upper Ground; the red wheel hubs are a nice touch but never appeared on subsequent Citaros, fixed or articulated.** *Author*

likelihood that passengers would simply stroll on without paying? TfL's faith in the honesty of the London bus passenger was not quite at its lowest ebb, as just the latest of fares trials involving the W7 was instituted on 17 October as a testbed for fares-free operation. Having tried and failed with 'Passright', by which those boarding the right-hand half of the entrance doors on this route's Volvo Olympians and MCW Metrobuses would be assumed to have a valid pass about their person, TfL now took a deep breath and gave the entire boarding complement the benefit of the doubt. The new twist here was the installation of roadside ticket machines along the W7's streets. At the same time, the evaluation of six artics on the 207 was commenced on 15 October, though these Volvo B10LAs and B7LAs diverted to Centrewest from other factions of FirstGroup, were only two-doored.

An unregistered Citaro G was one of Mercedes-Benz's exhibits at Coach & Bus at the NEC in October, and on 13/14 November, under trade plates 371 LD, was inspected by London General staff at Stockwell, Camberwell and Waterloo. The latter two of these three garages would go on to operate Citaro artics during their decade in service.

The awards were made on the basis of one final spot of tinkering, which saw the 501 taken off so that its Bank–London Bridge remit could be incorporated into an extension southward of the 141 from Moorgate. The 521, channelling passengers to and from Cannon Street as well as London Bridge and Waterloo, would take on its vehicles. However, London General had ordered the MALs, as they were to be classified, without taking the trouble to see whether they

Right: **Back then the debut of artics was not seen as a threat to Routemasters or other forms of British transport in London; they were ideally suited to the Red Arrows once the likelihood of fare evasion on a massive scale was phased in. Here is some publicity accompanying the introduction of the MALs onto the 507 and 521.** *Author's collection*

Red Arrow routes 507 & 521

Changes from 5 June 2002

More bus, less fuss

Buses are getting better

MAYOR OF LONDON

would fit into the Red Arrow routes' Waterloo base – thankfully, after a session with another demonstrator taken on loan in February 2002, it was discovered that they did. In any case the existing 11 would have to be thrown out to make room for the MALs' massive footprint, and since Stockwell covered it well enough on Saturdays and Sundays when Waterloo was obliged not to operate anyway, that was where it went from 25 May, in good time to prepare Waterloo.

The introduction of the MALs, put back from 27 April, had to drift further from 1 June since the third and fourth were declared Bank Holidays for the Queen's Golden Jubilee. Thus it was Wednesday 5 June 2002 that saw the 507 and 521's MALs replace the GLSs overnight. During May a number of them had been seen on driver training, and the rest, stored hitherto at Mercedes-Benz's Coventry premises, arrived at Waterloo on the evening of 31 May. This gave six days to add transfers, fleetnames, fleetnumbers and numberplates, and even blinds, these being delivered very late from the Danish manufacturer. The blind boxes were automatic, controlled by the driver, and thus required precision fitting to line up with chips, so the first couple of days had to be undertaken with temporary slipboards.

London General rather missed a trick with the livery, not adding the usual yellow tape band above the charcoal-grey skirt, and the only Red Arrow logos carried were in plain New Johnston Italic script on the smoked-glass panels above the windows in each half of the bus. The experimental Stenning-designed

logo carried uniquely by GLS 479 might have looked nice, but the glass-heavy design of the Citaros simply prohibited anything more exciting, especially when the proliferation of non-red liveries had fallen out of favour in recent years for fear of confusing passengers, who had enough on their plate as it was.

All the MALs, and indeed all but subsequent allocations to Stagecoach and First, would be registered by the manufacturers with Birmingham marks, underscoring the 'foreign-ness' of the vehicles that was already evident. Maintenance for London General's MALs was to be by Clarke's of Sydenham, some of the MALs arriving at Waterloo from this site.

In keeping with the old London Transport's anxiety to familiarise passengers with a new and revolutionary system of boarding in advance of a conversion, and mindful of the distinct failure it had suffered with making the passengers warm to the Merlin, Swift and DMS families, TfL and London General made it their business to publicise the open-boarding aspect of the Red Arrows ahead of time, even going so far as to emblazon adverts on the floor of Victoria, London Bridge and Waterloo stations.

Out went the Red Arrow GLSs without commemoration, despite these being definitely the last Leyland Nationals of any form in London service. Despite the wretched weather characterising Wednesday 5 June, and indeed, much of the rest of that year's summer, the replacement MALs got off to as reasonable a start as could be expected. Straightaway the commuting passengers

Right: **The nearside of Red Arrow MAL 13 (BX02 YYU) fighting its way through the rain of 5 June 2002 into Victoria bus station. All sorts of stickers and admonitions had to be applied to instruct the ever-dim passengers as to the correct way to use the buses, lest they just not bother paying at all (perish the thought!). However, the first day fell down in that the blinds were not ready, so slipboards had to be used, and being black on yellow they looked rather too much like the running numbers displayed by some of the less conscientious companies not derived from LBL.** *Author*

knew that there was something different about their new buses, over and above the Mayor making a public appearance in front of MAL 19, specially blinded for the first day. The only real problem was the rude shock to punters boarding expecting to put money in fareboxes, as they might have done on the MBAs, SMSs, LSs and GLSs since 1968, only to be turfed off, pointed to the roadside ticket machines and instructed to pay there, with no guarantee that such a device would work, or that the bus would stay there to wait while they did it! While the tear-off Saver tickets had to be shown to the driver so that he or she could tear off the business end, Travelcards and other passes absolved people from this rigmarole and, indeed any interaction with the driver; armed with these, you could simply board at any of the three doors. Very quickly, unfortunately, the less scrupulous of the London passenger body felt they could take their chances with not having to pay at all once they strolled on, with the likelihood of being collared by an inspector no greater than on any other bus – seemingly, befitting the weary old stereotype, there'd be no inspectors for weeks or months and then a glut of them!

In the same month as the Red Arrow conversion to cashless artic operation, a second route was awarded on this basis. By the end of 2001 the long trunk route 53 still operated from Oxford Circus out to the far south-east via the Elephant, Old Kent Road, New Cross, Greenwich and Woolwich before creeping round the back via Plumstead Common and finally descending the hill to terminate in its operating garage. Tranche 146, offered in September 2001, illustrated a new route 453 with as yet no indication as to whether this was going to either supplement or supplant the existing 53, but from its award to Stagecoach Selkent in June 2002 more details were publicised; commencing from Deptford Broadway, this route would accompany the 53 up the Old Kent Road and through the Elephant & Castle, County Hall and Westminster to Trafalgar Square, where it would assume the 53's roads alone to Oxford Circus before opening up a new link beyond to Marylebone via a left-hand turn at Great Portland Street. The award included a new night route N453 over the same roads, and it was envisaged that it would take 15 buses or so off the 53's PVR of 49 Tridents but add to capacity overall with about 30-35 artics.

Above: **The 521 was by now the only Red Arrow route operating into the City and as such was tremendously busy. Between the peaks shortworkings operated only as far as St Paul's, and on 6 June, by which time full blinds were now in use (though the St Paul's shorts unfortunately lacked via points), MAL 18 (BX02 YZB) calls at the first outbound stop from Waterloo. It's a shame London General didn't see fit to apply the yellow line separating the red livery from the grey skirt as on their other buses, and the vestigial Red Arrow branding is a disappointment to people who are into such embellishments.**
Author

The 453 and the next conversion to bendy buses were plotted out to a background of a distinctly Old Labour strategy of tax and spend, although Ken Livingstone had, in the interim, fallen out with the Labour Party over questions of orthodoxy, campaigning as an independent to be elected inaugural Mayor of the GLA. The 'tax' proportion that would hopefully unlock the money to 'spend' came in the form of what was dubbed the Congestion Charge, announced by the Mayor on 26 February 2002 for implementation from 17 March 2003. A legal challenge to Congestion Charging was mounted on 15 July 2002 by the City of Westminster and other units, but this was thrown out on 31 July by the High Court. Rather desperately, it cited the lack of consultation as a breach of human rights, a defence coming increasingly into use for just about any grievance you could care to offer at either end of the social spectrum.

Unlike previous attempts at collection, where cumbersome infrastructure like tollbooths and barriers had to be made space for by expensive road reconstruction, the C-Charge was thoroughly modern, supervised by a ring of high-res cameras mounted on gantries in a ring at the perimeter of the central London area selected. These were equipped with sophisticated software designed to read numberplates and either check them off against a register of pre-paid customers or log them for billing later, with the appropriate penalty for taking their time about it. The cost was an extremely extortionate £5 – far from enfranchising the lower-income brackets claimed to be supported by the populist Mayor, this did much to price them off the roads completely, while more monied echelons shrugged off what didn't amount to much of a hit on their everyday expenditure and got the roads to themselves. Forestalling popular resistance, the central facility for monitoring the camera gantries was based in Coventry, far from London. All this brought the capital a new and quickly familiar logo on signage and painted on roads - the white 'C' in its red circle. The gamble was that car commuters would not be able to weave around barriers or avoid

Left: **Like the back end of a bus; nothing particularly untoward here, the window being big enough still to see out of and the whole generally unencumbered by trends, as is the solid, conservative sort of Mercedes-Benz way that has worked so well for them in cars. There is, however, ample warning to cars coming up behind that artics are not to be trifled with, a notice of the outsize length being displayed on vehicles like MAL 12 (BX02 YYT), which is seen leaving Victoria on 24 June 2002.** *Author*

the charge, and the money generated would fund additional buses in their hundreds; hence the planning of new routes to skirt or cross the C-charge boundaries so that those unable or unwilling to pay it could, if nothing else were possible, at least park on the border and proceed into town one of the increased number of buses.

The splitting of the 36, however, had nothing to do with tendering; its existing contract with London Central applied from 27 May 2000 for five years, but in accordance with the development of Congestion Charging and the need for new links to take the expected strain of people priced out of cars, new route 436 was commissioned over its southeasternmost end. It had solid antecedents, the 36 group only having consolidated into the one route fairly recently, with the Hither Green and Brockley Rise components not replaced at all and the 136, derived from the old 36B, considerably weaker out to Grove Park than had been its MD-operated predecessor.

In June 2002 Stagecoach ordered forty Citaro Gs for the 453 and a month later Go-Ahead placed another order for thirty more MALs for the 436, which of course would be London Central vehicles. Mindful of the space problem that would ensue even at spacious Plumstead, Stagecoach anticipated the need to transfer some of its work to Catford once the 453 was assumed (disregarding the very long and wasteful dead run from Deptford that could not be done in service as a 53) and set about demolishing surplus buildings at Catford garage's south end.

Transport for London then proceeded to make a fatal mistake. With only thirty artics in service it all but predicted its future on them when, in an infamous pronunciation made at the Labour Party Conference in Blackpool on 30 September 2002, the Mayor announced the impending withdrawal of Routemasters. So much for being a party of the working class, Labour was about to throw several thousand of them – the conductors still working 629 vehicles on 22 routes – on the fire to service the party's latest politically-correct obsession, which this time was disabled access. Laudable in itself, the cost of achieving it was going to be massive, and at a potential risk to the tourist trade which was critical to London's survival. Like it or not, they, and they weren't the only ones, saw Routemasters as integral to and fundamental to not just London's culture, but Britain's as a whole. For all its plain-spoken efficiency as an appliance, there wasn't the slightest trace of culture or appeal in a crush-loading people-carrier from Germany, even with the undoubted badge cachet of Mercedes-Benz.

TfL rushed to implement damage control following media opprobrium, making it public in October that at least some Routemasters would remain in the capital, and that bendy buses were not intended as their wholesale replacements. Confidence in the technology being installed for the Congestion Charge was high enough that TfL did not foresee having to pull the scheme other than for a major malfunction, and held to the 17 February 2003 date of implementation.

Below: **Go-Ahead London's original seat moquette.**

CHAPTER FOUR

2003

Saturday 8 February 2003 was set as the date for the first non-Red Arrow artic conversion; already the first new routes and splits of existing ones across the Congestion Charge border had been implemented on 25 January so that passengers would be used to them in good time to be (hopefully) deluged by a wave of drivers priced out of their cars on 17 February. Accordingly, the 36 was cut back from Lewisham to New Cross; hardly an ideal traffic objective for passengers, who were already finding out the hard way, much as they had done during Reshaping, that they were being turfed off the routes they needed to get into town from far afield, frustratingly just short of where they needed to go, only

to be made to wait, board and pay a second time. New Cross, however, was where the garage was for both the 36 and 436 and thus convenient for the operator rather than the passengers. The 36 lost 24 of its RMs, now fielding 26 of them on a 7.5min frequency over the whole route without the four-part overlap as previous; the 436 in effect occupied the southern overlap with a six-minute peak-hour frequency between Paddington and Lewisham, using 26 buses.

Built alongside Stagecoach's order in Mannheim starting in November and shipped to the UK from the third week of December onwards, London Central's route 436 complement comprised MALs 32-61, all registered by Evobus with West Midlands

Right: **Despite the hacking away in 1986 of a key central London section that ruined its ability to cross town, the 53 remained a tremendously busy trunk route that penetrated further out into the suburbs than comparable routes with better turning points along the route. OPO had come in 1988 and an express accompaniment had come and gone, and by the turn of the century low-floor buses had settled in the form of TA-class Dennis Tridents from Stagecoach Selkent's Plumstead garage. Here in Woolwich on 20 April 2003 is TA 133 (V133 MEV), just before the unfortunate decision by Stagecoach to dump its time-honoured London Transport-derived class codes for an all-numeric system that not only failed to stick in the memory, but contradicted itself repeatedly.** *Author*

Left: **Like the 53, the 36 had seen greater days, though in this case Routemasters had managed to survive in charge and the paring back was from the southeast direction. All projections further out of town than Lewisham had been discontinued or folded into other local routes, and the intent of the forthcoming 436 was to cut it back further so that it terminated rather conveniently at New Cross garage, which had since the relocation of Peckham in 1993 been the 36's base. Re-engining with Scania units and some bodily freshening-up, though not to the extent of the official refurbishments, had taken the 36's RM fleet through to the turn of the millennium, and on 28 March 2002 we see RM 1033 (DSL 540, ex-33 CLT) at Peckham bus station, once Peckham garage.** *Author*

marks spanning three series, BD, BL and BN. Still seating 49, the posted standing capacity of these was five fewer (86) by comparison with the Red Arrow motors. Once again the passengers quickly found out they were onto a good thing, ignoring the roadside ticket machines that had been installed along the Peckham Road corridor in recent weeks.

A week later on Saturday 15 February, the 453 was introduced – but the first hiccup to the otherwise fairly orderly introduction of artics forced this route to make its bow with TAs, owing to the fact that not all the artics were likely to be present by the introduction date, and all of them were needed at once to implement cashless operation; the differing payment formats meant that buses couldn't be phased in. As had been planned for, however, the 54 and 202 were transferred to Catford to make room at Plumstead for the unwieldy bulk of the 'MAs'.

Stagecoach's order, built from November onwards and delivered to Evobus before onward dispatch to Plumstead, was intended to form an MA class under Stagecoach Selkent, but the introduction of a national numbering system from 6 January 2003 brought them into an all-numeric series starting at 23001. The first five were licensed with the 52-registrations of the batch booked for all thirty-five, the rest crossing the 1 March line denoting 03-plates, and all had area indicators booked at the Sidcup LVLO (which after this point only ever seemed to issue buses with 'LX'). The red buses had the blue skirt introduced in 2001 but not the 'beach ball' stripes at the rear, which would

have been fouled by the large expanse of glass. Inside was Stagecoach's standard red floor with orange paisleys, blue seating with red and orange 'beach ball' motifs woven in and orange handrails. Seating capacity was AB49T plus 86 standing.

Left: **Accompanying the squadron introduction of bendy buses was the new method by which they'd be funded, since revenue from on-bus fares paid was not going to even be approaching 100%. The Congestion Charge threw a ring around part of central London more obsessively monitored than the old Ring of Steel, whose police checkpoints quickly lost their personnel as budgets were cut. Here is an example of the kind of sign that would greet drivers approaching the border, with little leeway either to beat the cameras by sneaking in early or to do the same by driving out of the zone late. The 'C' logo, emblazoned in stretched form on road surfaces as well as on signs and publicity, became somewhat iconic, if that thoroughly hackneyed word may be used in the ironic sense that should fit the rest of this account!** *Creative Commons*

The 453 and N453 took on their intended buses and method of payment (or not, as the unfortunate inevitability turned out) on Saturday 15 March, bringing the number of artic routes in London to four day and one night; the 453's conversion in the small hours saw TAs still in service. Physical difficulties were evident at both ends of the route, unfortunately; its stand at Marylebone station (which did, however, provide a new link) normally belonged to the 2, which had to be thrown out back to its former terminus at Baker Street, while at Deptford there was as yet no turning circle. New Cross garage, which sufficed perfectly well for short turns in London Transport days, now belonged to a rival company, and the next closest turn involved making a circuit of Blackheath; the buses might as well have continued on to Woolwich and Plumstead as before,

for all the trouble that would have been worth. Therefore its buses were sent dead down Brookmill Road to Lewisham, but TfL completely failed to take the hint and liven up what would have been an enormously useful new link. It wasn't until much later that a small stand was hacked out beside the DLR's bridge over Deptford High Road.

The introduction of Congestion Charging proved relatively trouble-free; it brought about a reduction for the moment in traffic volumes (albeit with skewed statistics due to the implementation of the scheme during half-term) and a 10% increase in bus ridership. All of it had to be paid for, of course, and even the government baulked at Ken Livingstone's greed, cutting his request for an increase to the proportion of Council Tax earmarked for the GLA for the 2003-04 budget from 34% to 29.1%. Simultaneously, plans were set in train to commence the controversial and unpopular removal of the Routemaster fleet from its twenty remaining routes. While the 15 and 11 were first to succumb, the conversion of the third route (23) was tied to the fate of the 18. Awarded to and retained by First in April 2003 as part of Tranche 162 issued in August 2002, this long route had perhaps had a better innings with doored buses than had many other central London crew services subjected to DMs in the 1970s – and perhaps due in no small part to the sad fact that along its Harrow Road corridor, many of the people to be found there were unremittingly violent towards bus crews and had to be deterred from their plans by closed doors rather than open platforms. The 18 was one-manned on 1 February 1986, its City leg already having been torn away, and by the time it was tendered its terminus was settled at Euston.

Right: **With the Oyster card only in its infancy, a second front of off-bus payment (other than Travelcards bought in shops) came in the form of these roadside ticket machines; personal observations on the 436's first day were of puzzled boarders being ordered straight off with a finger pointed at one of these machines, only to be left behind as the bus closed its doors and set off! That would teach them to board subsequently at either of the other two doors and not worry about paying at all; some drivers, relieved by not having to deal with passengers' unlimited stupidity any longer and indeed incentivised by the artic drivers' premium, didn't open the front doors at all. Another personal observation saw one of these unloved (though, to be fair, generally reliable) machines rifled for its entire contents by a tramp in Oxford Street, with not a hint of opposition. This one at Waterloo was photographed on 22 September 2000, pre-dating artics there by over eighteen months.** *Author*

Red Arrow MAL 12 was borrowed by TfL on 22 January to carry out a trial over the 18's roads as part of a process that saw the 94 similarly surveyed (without success, owing to the tight turn at the Acton Green end that was hard enough for its existing RMLs) and MAL 28 evaluated over the roads intended for the East London Transit scheme in Ilford and Barking, which if successful could become a tram. Artics were seen as the next best thing to trams, being long and low-floor throughout.

Also in April 2003, the 149 was awarded to and retained by Arriva London North on the basis of conversion to artic during the period of its contract. From the issue of its tender in September 2002 under Tranche 164, the route was intended for splitting regardless of the final form of its operation,

Left: **A little bit of a hitch to the 453's introduction was that not all of Stagecoach Selkent's new artics were ready in time for the 15 February 2003 launch date. No matter; it was no big deal simply to set it going for its first four weeks with the amount of TAs that it would have displaced anyway. Rather blocking the Whitehall stop on 16 February is 17161 (V161 MEV), and it wouldn't be the last time double-deckers appeared on the 453 during its tenure with bendies.** *Author*

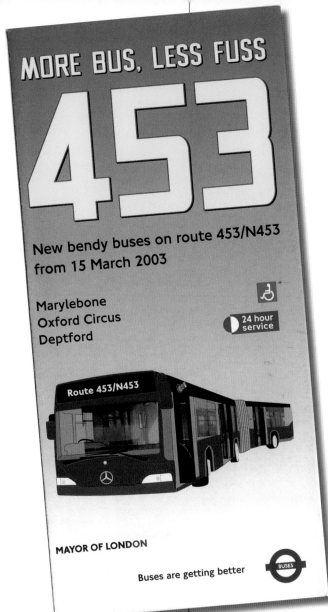

MORE BUS, LESS FUSS
453

New bendy buses on route 453/N453
from 15 March 2003

Marylebone
Oxford Circus
Deptford

24 hour service

Route 453/N453

MAYOR OF LONDON

Buses are getting better

Above: **The surfeit of glass on the Citaro design precludes much innovation in terms of livery unless you start going over it, which antagonises passengers who need to be able to see out. Thus the Stagecoach artics for the 453 lacked the 'beach ball' swirls that normally went over the rearmost couple of bays. They also adopted numeric fleetnumbers after the first two were coded in an MA class, and here at the Marylebone Station stand on 15 March, the first day of artic operation on the 453, is Plumstead's 23017 (LX03 HCY). The leaflet for the conversion is at left.** *Author*

Below: **The first southbound stop at Whitehall is a reliable pitch between one and two in the afternoon during spring and summer, and that's where we see Plumstead's 23025 (LX03 HCU) on 26 July 2003.** *Author*

losing its northernmost section between Edmonton Green and Ponders End to a new 349, which would overlap as far south as Stoke Newington but provide no new links (even when one in the direction of Hackney Central was just standing there begging)

In May First headed off likely problems with accommodation by purchasing a site near Willesden Junction for the operation of the 18, with room for expansion. On 5 June it was announced that 32 Citaro Gs had been ordered, which would be introduced shortly after the commencement of its new contract, a date which moved repeatedly but which was finalised as 13 September. Conversion would be accompanied by the OPO conversion of the 23, which would be executed using the 18's TNs until the balance of its new TALs arrived, and both programmes were implemented on 15 November. The First London Citaros were numbered ECA 3001-3032 and the first few entered service labelled as such before FirstGroup's fleet-renumbering programme reached the capital in December and rechristened them EA 11031-11032, E standing in either case for Evobus and A for articulated in as much as class codes represented anything as such within this company. Physical renumbering

Left: **The leaflet for Oyster cards, the genuine game-changer that at last sped up boarding times.**

Above: **For 2002 and 2003 only, artics were new enough and unthreatening enough to be welcome at Cobham's Spring Gathering. To be fair, a need was pressing to provide an accessible option not only for wheelchair-based enthusiasts but for those who couldn't or wouldn't walk the entirety of the perimeter at Brooklands. Thus on 6 April 2003 brand new 23010 (LX03 HCJ) helped out on the 477 and 499 link routes; at five past three it is seen opposite the museum. Typically, after a long spell of splendid weather, Cobham day proved overcast!** *Author*

Below: **The interior introduced by Stagecoach in 2000 to accompany its new liveries featured some fierce colour clashes, with blue, red and orange all fighting for visual prominence.**

Right: **Rail replacement eventually calls all London buses, no matter the class or capacity, but on Saturday 19 July 2003 Waterloo's MAL 14 (BX02 YYC) has been pressed into service while the Red Arrows are sleeping, carrying extra passengers from Charlton station to the Millennium Dome for a music festival. The slipboards (one of which is affixed rather unsafely in the middle of the windscreen) denote it as an adjunct to the 486.** *Author*

Below: **The 18 prior to artic conversion didn't need any cutting back, as that had already happened during the route's long decline post-Reshaping and culminating with its own OPO conversion. The route had now settled on a Euston–Sudbury pattern up and down the Harrow Road mostly on its own, and since 1999 had been operated with Dennis Tridents like TN 974 (X974 HLT) seen on 3 August 2003 making its first right turn out of Euston bus station into the Euston Road.** *Author*

took until the following July to implement. The subsidiary geographical fleetnames were dropped on 6 December 2003 and Willesden Junction's EAs never carried any – whether they would have still counted as Gold Arrow or been physically closer to Challenger territory will never be known! All were plain red, not taking the white and grey willow-leaf stripes familiar on other CentreWest and Capital vehicles, and the interior was First's sickly purple and turquoise affair.

Arriva London North now firmed up its intentions with the 149, first borrowing London General MAL 30 for a survey over the route on 17 June and finding the arrow-straight nature of this route eminently suitable for the buses at least, never mind the poor creatures expected to travel on them. TfL cleared the route for articulated operation in August and an order was placed in September for 29 Citaro Gs. The 149's new contract commenced on 18 October, with conversion to artic pencilled in for the following spring.

Two crucial developments characterised 2003, to soften the blow that the Congestion Charge was not actually bringing in the bonanza of money that had been expected so eagerly, with the accompanying knock-on effects on future funding and bus orders.

Left: **Like the 18, the 149 had one major artery to serve, only the roads where it went after that being of more interest. RM-operated since its creation in 1961 out of trolleybus route 649, DMs had come and gone, so had RCLs and eventually the second spell with Routemasters gave way to OPO Ms in 1987 and it was only in the last four years that low-floor buses had appeared, comprising a drip-feed of DLAs like DLA 207 (W407 VGJ), which is seen at Monument on 16 August 2003. North of Edmonton Green, the 149 would cede its roads to a new and rather perfunctory 349 that added nothing of importance.** *Author*

Left: **Stagecoach chose not to apply their rear swirls to their artics, and nor did First London add its willow leaves when the 18 was converted; they might have looked quite cheerful on the otherwise bland and unenticing all-red. On 15 November, its first day in service, ECA 3026 (LK53 FCE) demonstrates that the 18's stand and first stop at Euston has been moved round the corner to the nearest available straight sixty feet of kerb. The route was now operating from a new garage at Willesden Junction (WJ), but you'd never know it due to First's recalcitrance in displaying proper garage codes. A duty number is carried in the windscreen, but it's fallen down.** *Author*

Below left: **The palpable desperation of companies to force their uniqueness down passengers' throats for their custom was nowhere clearer than in some of the interiors they specified; if First's reputation wasn't shaky enough by the turn of the century, they really cemented it with this purple and turquoise horror of hideous clashing colours. This is looking towards the front of one from the seats over the third axle. When it was realised that the seat moquette was asymmetrical and thus would not match from seat to seat, it was revised slightly for the better, but First London's artics did not last long enough to receive it.** *Jack Marian*

Above: **The moquette on First London artics' seats.**

Above: **And on their ceiling panels, with purple accompaniment.**

Right: **Ostensibly arrow-straight from beginning to end, the 207 road suffers from bottlenecks that hamper the buses on their eleven-mile slog from Shepherds Bush to Uxbridge and back. Although there are wide-open multi-lane sections like through Hillingdon and past Ealing Hospital, the pinch points at Southall and West Ealing will put paid to any notions of reliability without having to cut the route into overlapping sections, which is inevitably what happened to the 207 and which would form the basis for its permanent split into two routes. After thirteen years of Ms following OPO conversion, Tridents appeared in 2000 in the form of TNLs; TNL 32926 (W926 VLN), having added thirty-two thousand to its fleetnumber following First's 2003 renumbering, calls at Ealing Common on 19 March 2005, two weeks before the conversion to artics.** *Author*

On 26 June the first Oyster cards were sold to the public; this contactless form of smartcard payment would achieve enormous success. Finally, after thirty years of abject failure to cut down boarding times through either automatic fare collection or paper passes, this was the Holy Grail that would not only provide vital details of boarding patterns in the interest of route maintenance, but, unfortunately, provide a more solid case than hitherto for the removal of crew operation.

Then, on 30 August, a cashless zone was implemented in a section of the West End, passengers being expected to have passes, Oyster cards, Saver tickets or have bought a ticket from the roadside machines plumbed in on the affected area's streets in the previous months. The inevitable solution was to go cap-in-hand again by announcing plans on 23 October to extend the Congestion Charge westwards in 2006 and, sooner or later, increase the charge itself. The first anniversary of the Charge was accompanied by an RAC report that traffic speeds in central London had increased from 2.9 mph to 7.4 mph – significant, but hardly earth-shattering!

On 26 September TfL awarded the 207 to its incumbent First London as an artic service. Issued under Tranche 169A in November 2002 as an early tender with an eye to its likely reconfiguration pending approval of the Mayor's West London Transit tram idea, this route reverted to its original contract term commencing at the end of 2004, but would be split nonetheless, its already autonomous western section taking the number 427 as a double-deck service. The main 207, terminating at Hayes By-Pass roundabout, would thus also need a new base, neither Uxbridge nor Acton Tram Depot being able to accommodate bendies and Greenford, which had operated the trial artics two years earlier, too full. As with Willesden Junction, TfL was responsible for locating new premises. A site at Gypsy Corner, North Acton was sought but planning permission failed to progress, and until this was sorted out no order could be placed. Structural changes were pretty much ruled out on artic routes, though on 13 December London General amended the 521 so that its peak-hour shorts from Waterloo to St Paul's were extended to London Bridge in line with the main service.

By the end of 2003 there were 128 artics in service on five routes, with three more routes scheduled for their introduction – all so far on generally sensible corridors that were either wide enough to physically suit the buses, or with an alternative form of bus travel that artics complemented rather than supplanted. Unfortunately, hereafter, Transport for London couldn't resist the temptation of falling headlong into the same old trap that had beset its London Transport predecessor of leaping on a gimmick and then applying it increasingly inappropriately to make it

pay for itself, refusing to admit failure until gargantuan amounts of money had been wasted, for fear of having to spend even more to set things right again. From Merlins and Swifts in the late 1960s through DMSs in the 1970s, minibuses in the 1980s and full-size single-deckers in the 1990s, successive administrations had made the same mistakes again and again, seemingly totally unable to draw from historical lessons in the belief that they could re-invent the wheel. Such was the award of the 73 in November on the basis of artics.

Right: **Unremittingly busy despite the far quicker option of the Central Line paralleling it, the 25 could not have been worse suited to artics. Even the TN-class Tridents put on in 1999 were patently inadequate with only 59 seats each, and within a year new TALs had taken over; but still the route needed more buses. TAL 946 (W946 ULL) is seen opposite Bow Road station on 4 June 2004.** *Author*

Below: **Once the route with the highest PVR in London and stretching clear across town, the 12 was mercilessly hacked and hacked until by 2003 it was a shadow of its former self and operated by just the one garage, Camberwell. It was selected for one-manning with bendies, which would see off venerable Routemasters like RML 2469 (JJD 469D) caught at the Elephant & Castle on 20 October 2003.** *Author*

You couldn't get much more inappropriate a route for bendy buses than the 73; serving Oxford Street throughout its length, it was the busiest bus route in London with a PVR of 55 RMLs. Under artics, the PVR was set to shrink to 41; assuming a Citaro G seated 49 and an RML seated 72, that was a reduction in seating capacity of 50% – totally unacceptable for people having to slog into town from the north-west and/or pile on in the length of Oxford Street. To say nothing of the clearances, which in Stoke Newington in particular were perilously close even

for Routemasters. TfL had become used to having to spend the money to knock out traffic obstructions and lengthen bus stops to accommodate artics, and saw the 73 road as no different. In all, TfL was taking an enormous gamble with the 73, and from this point on heads were shaken in disbelief everywhere as artics turned from being an expensive but reasonably plausible novelty to battering rams pushing the modern TfL's politically-correct ethos aggressively into the faces of the people who paid through the nose to maintain it in business.

Left: **One of the most enduring insults that have been applied to the bendy bus is one likening them to airside transfer vehicles, these being a staple of low-budget package holidays before the development of air bridges to take passengers seamlessly from departure lounge to aircraft. Long after such vehicles had ceased to be used airside, there was still ample opportunity for inter-terminal transport as airports grew and grew, and in 2003 Menzies took ten Scania CN94UA artics for staff transport. It was a good call, as Heathrow mushroomed in the decade following, creating Terminal 5 where B 33 (YN53 GHA) is seen on 4 April 2010. That was the year that Menzies bought eleven more, though the chassis designation by then was CN280UA.** *Jimmy Sheng*

Above: **Nothing looks particularly out of the ordinary for New Cross's MAL 58 (BL52 ODS) as it proceeds along the Vauxhall Bridge Road in September 2003, but in six months this and two other route 436 artics would be history, burnt out in circumstances controversial enough to urge a rethink on continuing bendy conversions.** *Haydn Davies*

CHAPTER FIVE

2004

Not content with having compromised the 73's future with its selection for artic conversion, TfL closed out 2003 by awarding two further critical central London services on the same basis. The 25's eleven-mile slog had much of its roads to itself as it paralleled the Central Line between Mile End and Stratford, and no matter how many buses were thrown at it, sucked them up and still needed more. At the present time it operated forty Tridents from First Capital, a PVR which had been hoisted from thirty only a year earlier, and the buses replaced by longer versions seating more. This time the contract involved an operator change, which would restore it to Stagecoach East London with a commencement date of 26 June 2004. Replacement of forty 68-seat TALs or TNLs

with 37 artics seating 49 would lower seating capacity from 2,720 to 1,813 (34%).

The concurrent award of the 12 to its incumbent London Central represented the second direct conversion from Routemaster to artics; with intent from as soon as possible following its contract assumption date of 31 July 2004, 29 artics would replace 37 RMLs, though this 47% drop in seats would be ameliorated slightly by withdrawing the 12 between Oxford Circus and Notting Hill Gate and adding that section to another double-deck route.

In December 2003 Arriva ordered 47 Citaro Gs for the 73 and Stagecoach ordered 42 for the 25. So far operators had plumped solely for the Citaro G, none being tempted by Scania's articulated N94UA/CN94UA

Right: **The basic Mercedes-Benz Citaro lent itself to any application; as well as artics, there were the thirty fuel cell examples operating in trios in ten cities from 2003. London's contingent comprised First London ESQs 64991-64993, of which ESQ 64993 (LK53 MBV) is seen at Oxford Circus on 19 January 2004. Their use on the 25 alongside the existing TALs and TNLs was something of a test run prior to artics, as well as evaluating the complicated fuel-cell gear, but was broadly successful, the biggest deal being the no-emissions aspect. After the 25 was lost to Stagecoach they moved over to the RV1, and although they were not to last much longer, formed a very small toehold for fuel-cell buses in London that today is exemplified by Wright-based WSH-class vehicles, again based on the RV1.** *Author*

Left: **So far, the gradual phasing of artics onto routes had not directly threatened Routemasters down on the ground other than the reduction in PVR on the 36, but the fire problems encountered early in 2004 were devastating to the Citaro's reputation in the long term. Here is what is left of MAL 36 (BD52 LNN) after its rapid consumption by fire in Park Lane on 3 December 2003. On 7 February 2004 MAL 51 was also destroyed by fire, and when MAL 58 became the third New Cross Citaro to go up in flames only six weeks later and an Arriva example was simultaneously destroyed on delivery, full-blown panic set in. It wasn't just the London ones that were doing it either, for all the satisfaction it would have given some critical parties (including this one) to blame the immolations on the exhausting stop-start traffic conditions of the capital.**
PA Images

offering, examples of which had been milling about on the edge of Heathrow's forthcoming Terminal 5 since November under the aegis of Menzies. They similarly failed to look further into the possibilities offered by Evobus's fuel-cell project, which in conjunction with ten major cities around the world evaluated three fuel-cell Citaros each, though the £1.2m cost per bus was undoubtedly a deterrent. London's participation from 14 January 2004 comprised three operated by First on a supplementary service on the 25, based at Hackney where a set of above-ground hydrogen tanks was installed specially for them. Evobus didn't stop there with the Citaro, showing to the Association of Train Operating Companies (ATOC) a 'road train' conversion intended to form a plausible alternative to expensive railway branch lines as tried out in Germany.

The generally positive experience with the 25's three ESQs and the versatility of the Citaro design in general should have marked it out, as sales worldwide corroborated, as a competent and reliable vehicle worthy of being chosen by operators in London as well as across the globe. However, in London, disaster struck, not once but three times (nobody mention the old 'three at once' trope which will forever saddle London's buses). At 6.15 in the morning on 3 December, New Cross's MAL 36 caught fire in the Edgware Road north of Marble Arch while on the 436 and was completely destroyed. The road was closed for several hours while the remains were scraped up onto a low-loader and taken away. On 7 February 2004 MAL 51 demised in a similar manner on the same route, losing

its entire rear beyond the concertina section, and on 20 March MAL 58 went up in flames in Park Lane at twenty past six in the evening while operating northbound, the outcome total destruction in just four minutes, assisted by a strong southwesterly wind that made the smoke so fierce that it activated alarms in the Hilton Hotel, a considerable distance away across the road!

MAL 36's charred remains reposed at the Penge premises of Queen's Motors until 21 February when it and MAL 51 were spirited away somewhere out of sight for investigation into the cause of the accident, believed at that point to be an engine fault. But the destruction of MAL 58, and a further accident at 2.15 in the morning of 15 March involving Arriva London North MA 40, which caught fire on the M25 near Waltham Cross while being sent down to Tottenham Marshes from Evobus in Coventry, prompted all-out panic. While first resolving to check all Citaros, both rigid and articulated, every night, while Mercedes-Benz agreed to a programme of fire-suppression equipment fitment and the London Fire Brigade and Vehicle Inspectorate were called in to provide an independent review of the three London Central fires, TfL then ordered all Citaros taken off the road on 24 March on advice from Mercedes-Benz.

The three operators of the 151 bendy buses already in London service, plus two more that operated rigid Citaros, had to scramble into action anything they could get hold of during the roughly two weeks that it took fifty Mercedes-Benz engineers brought over from Germany to inspect the compressors on

Left: **Haters of the bendy delighted in TfL's distress; for now, the truly hardcore of the critics were mostly confined to enthusiasts who, via TLB and other inside sources, were tipped off ahead of time that several more routes were pencilled in for conversion, but where London's image was concerned, this felt like the city getting its own back on its faceless bureaucrats. For what could kick Ken Livingstone and his about-face policies more squarely in the teeth than the emergency deployment of Routemasters on the Red Arrow route 507? Because until it was figured out quite what the hell was going wrong with the Citaros, all of them were pulled out of service. Here at Victoria on 25 March is RML 2725 (SMK 725F), snatched from the private-hire department at London Central, which also made RM 9 available. This pair combined to usher out the 12's last day with Routemasters on 5 November.** *Author*

each bus, unblock them where needed and replace them altogether in some cases. Delight ensued among enthusiasts and the press alike as Go-Ahead was forced to press some of its Commercial Services Routemasters into service on the 507, undoubtedly turning on its head a policy stance which was beginning to go terribly badly for TfL. Darts from London General sales stock stood in for the single-deck-restricted 521; the 18 was covered by spare Westbourne Park (and Alperton) Volvo B7TLs and Tridents with assistance from Metroline at one point, while the 436 was suspended entirely in favour of an increased service on the 36 until PVLs were gathered, and at Selkent the 453 was covered by other garages' Tridents, bolstered by new examples plucked from their delivery runs to Stagecoach East Midland at Chesterfield.

The problem was traced to a surprisingly familiar source; oil leaks onto hot exhaust manifolds from pipe fractures had also taken out DMSs in sizeable numbers, but then again the Fleetlines weren't working with feeble underpowered engines boosted insufficiently by overworked turbochargers for the sake of obsessively stringent emissions legislation.

Above left: **The 521 of course couldn't take double-deckers because of its run under the Aldwych tunnel, so a handful of Darts were gathered together. This one is DMS 11 (T272 RMY, ex-101 CLT), normally the property of Bexleyheath for one of the B-routes in that area, and it is seen arriving at Waterloo with slipboards in the windscreen.** *Steve Maskell*

Left: **The reappearance of double-deckers on the 18 was no surprise to its passengers only five months on, but there weren't quite enough TALs to spare from the 23, which had been one-manned at the same time, so Metroline were deputised to help out and here at Euston on 25 March is Volvo B7TL VPL 187 (Y187 NLK) otherwise from the 52's allocation.** *Author*

Right: Volvo Olympian VN 99 (T899 KLF) from Alperton was another double-decker deputised to help out on the 18; two sheets of A4 with a number '18' printed have had to serve as blinds in this Euston view. *Steve Maskell*

Below right: Having spent its first month with TAs, the 453 did it again while its artics were checked over and fitted with fire-suppression equipment as per the other companies' examples. Loans from both East London and Selkent were gathered in by Plumstead, and those coming from Catford were the shorter-wheelbase 9.9m examples previously known as TASs. On 26 March 2004 17542s (LY02 OAO) is seen at Pall Mall East. Makeshift blinds stuck to the windscreen with Blu-Tack had to be used, as new blind sets for Plumstead now omitted the 453 with the intention that double-deckers should never be allowed to substitute for artics. *Author*

Bottom: As well as the mixed bag of 'TA' and 'TAS' loans, the 453 was bolstered by Tridents requisitioned from Stagecoach's provincial companies. They could be distinguished not only by their national livery but by their low-height configuration and, perhaps most helpfully, LED blinds allowing the route details to be displayed properly. Here in the Old Kent Road is 18126 (YN04 KGP) from East Midland. *Steve Maskell*

Arriva's incomers weren't affected, as the damage to MA 40 was traced to its driver ignoring a low coolant alarm which prompted the engine to overheat and seize; this batch's compressor pipes had already been improved as part of ongoing modifications. Once all Citaros had gone back into service by 9 April, the fire-suppression kits ordered under warranty (and there would have been hell to pay if they hadn't been!) arrived and all operators, including Arriva, sent their buses to Walworth to have them fitted, leading to double-deckers standing in once again on routes 18, 149 (once converted on the 24th),

436, 453 and normal Citaro-operated route RV1 until the end of the month; TfL allowed double-deckers to appear on artic routes no later than 1 May. The kits would dump water or powder on the engine if temperatures rose too far, indicated in the cab by an alarm that, if sounded, would warn the driver to stop and cut the engine as a first resort.

Prior to the big withdrawal, the numbers at New Cross were made up when a Citaro G from demonstrator stock was put into service on the 436; white-painted BU53 ZWV, with Mercedes emblems over the windows, differed by not having a centre door and featuring dot-matrix blinds. It lasted until August. An alternative chassis was also evaluated from 13 February in the shape of Hispano Habit-bodied Volvo B7LA FJ53 LZX

of AB48T+75 capacity, painted in the red and charcoal of Go-Ahead London and carrying the fleetnumber X 62; this stayed at New Cross till 10 March and then spent a month with Waterloo on the 507 and 521. But despite the nerves now being experienced with the Citaro chassis, a sentiment shared in Europe where at least five of the vehicles had suffered similar fires, the choice of bus for artic contracts remained exclusively Mercedes-Benz.

On the night of 19/20 March the N453 lost its 'N' prefix as part of a bungled attempt to standardise day and night routeings before it was realised that the N-routes could not disappear altogether due to not all of them being identical to their daytime numbers by any means.

Barring the mishap with MA 40, Arriva London North's artics for the 149 started to arrive in Britain in January for pre-service checks at Evobus in Coventry, which booked their registrations before sending them on to storage at Arriva's recently-acquired overspill storage site at Tottenham Marshes during February. Like the First London examples, a concession was made to the surfeit of glass on the buses by omitting the Arriva 'cow horn' and just applying the yellow tape band at skirt level; interior was Arriva standard with black floor, bluish-turquoise seats and yellow handrails. Perhaps mindful of the carnage meted out south of the river, it borrowed Stagecoach Selkent's 23029 on 3 February to make doubly sure that it fitted the Hertford Road. On 1 May the 73's new contract took effect with its existing RMLs, the conversion to artic scheduled to follow. By now contracts meant a lot less than they might have done, it being easy to change the allocated vehicle type in mid-stream, as was being done to several of the Routemaster routes in order to get rid of the buses come what may; otherwise, if contract dates had

been strictly adhered to, the 14 would have been the last Routemaster-operated route on 22 November 2007.

Space continued to be a problem, Stagecoach Selkent establishing an outstation at North Greenwich with capacity for ten of the 453's artics from 15 March 2004; drivers would still book on at Plumstead and then be ferried to their steeds. North Greenwich was just as far away from line of route as Deptford, unfortunately, so the problem was literally shifted elsewhere.

On 24 April the 149 was duly converted from DLA operation to artics after five weeks of training (which included forays along the 73 road) and the throughput of the MAs into Walworth from 13 April for fitment of fire-suppression equipment. The route was curtailed as planned at Edmonton Green and the night service (previously known as N149) between the same termini being taken up simultaneously. Once again there had to be a garage change, Enfield giving way to a confusing setup whereby Edmonton (EC) housed the MAs but Stamford Hill (SF) drivers drove them; as the Lea Valley Reservoir separated one setup geographically from the next, ferry operations had to be mounted over the several miles in between, wasting more precious and expensive fuel. While every chance was given the passengers with the installation of Oyster card readers at all three doors and the introduction shortly after of Oyster Pre-Pay, the 149 quickly vaulted to the top of the fare-evasion pile, an astonishing eleven per cent being recorded not bothering to pay – and that was the ones that were caught! Worst-case scenarios, not all of which can have been malicious speculation by those ranged in opposition to bendy bus operation, were putting the level of fare evasion at an appalling 75%! If that wasn't bad enough, the roadside ticket machines made easy

Left: **The 149's first-day service under artics had faltered sufficiently by mid-afternoon to necessitate short turns to Dalston, Downham Road, performed in this instance by MA 4 (BX04 MXA), caught at Stamford Hill Broadway.** *Author*

cashpoints for those with the wherewithal to jemmy them, the author having observed such an individual shamelessly cleaning one out in Oxford Street. TfL and the Mayor alike expressed public displeasure with them, halting further roadside installations and placing their faith, quite rightly as it turned out, in Oyster cards instead. In the short term, the penalty fare was doubled to £10.

If there was hope, it lay in the Mayor. The second election for such a post took place on 10 June 2004, but Ken Livingstone, restored to membership of the Labour Party on 6 January

and running under its platform (so to speak) was re-elected; not only the conversions to bendy bus, but the removal of Routemasters, would continue.

Mercedes-Benz were magnanimous enough to supply like-for-like replacements to London Central for the three destroyed, and they were delivered in May, June and July respectively as second incarnations of MALs 36, 51 and 58, though the 04-registrations gave them away. Early deliveries to Arriva London North in time for the 73 continued into May, though fire suppression kits were

Left: **One might mutter about the morality of reusing a dead relative's name, but it wasn't seen as suspect practice to effectively cover up the loss of the three New Cross MALs by giving their replacements the same fleetnumbers. The second MAL 51 (BU04 EZK), distinguishable from its charbroiled predecessor only by the 04-registration, entered service on 11 June 2004 and is seen on the 436 at Victoria on 28 August.** *Author*

Below: **All conversions and route transfers suffer first-day nerves, but the 25's first day with artics was catastrophic. By mid-afternoon buses were running in fives, few of them were penetrating west of Holborn Circus, and every single one of them was groaning with standing loads right up to the windscreen, illegally blocking the driver's view out. It was difficult to determine quite what the public of London had done or said that was so bad as to be punished with this ludicrously inadequate form of transport. The buses themselves were 23036-23077, forty-two more Citaro Gs identical to their Selkent forebears and exemplified at Holborn on the first day by 23076 (LX04 LCV).** *Author*

Right: **The driver of 23061 (LX04 LBV) working as WA31 on 26 June is still getting to grips with the dimensions of his steed in this Stratford view. For all the sixty-foot length of the artics, they were surprisingly manoeuvrable if kept in a straight line; the driver has swung way out into the left-hand turn in the belief that doing otherwise would have grated him against the railings, but if he'd stayed on an even keel the rear portion would simply have followed the front over the exact path it would have taken. Photographers that were used to the entire bus filling their viewfinders could find themselves nonplussed by angles like this, in which half the bus appeared to have vanished out of sight!** *Author*

not yet available; the 149's batch had to be detached from service at the same time to have their fuel pumps changed, buses being taken off at London Bridge and driven off to Walworth, where the work was done. Work like this was made easier at Willesden Junction by the opening of two extra-long inspection pits.

Rear adverts were an established fixture in London by now, but the first to be applied to artics were to three Willesden Junction EAs in May; rather than advertising a product, they advised against gun crime on behalf of the Metropolitan Police.

Quite a bit had to be done to prepare the 25 for its new lot under artics from 26 June 2004; stand space was made at Hainault Street in Ilford for the behemoths by taking out five of the routes that terminated there; the 129 was withdrawn altogether so that extensions to the 128 and 150 could take up that route's Claybury and Becontree Heath legs respectively, while the 167 was ejected round the corner and the 296 pulled back to the Sainsbury's stand short of the town centre proper. The terminus at Oxford Circus also had to be revised so that the buses approached the stand from the wider streets to the south rather than chancing the direct right turn into Holles Street. In the interests of standardisation, the N25 was withdrawn east of Ilford and lost its 'N' to accompany reallocation to Stagecoach with the day route. Again there was a new garage to reckon with; Waterden Road (WA) near Stratford, and indeed across the road from the existing Stratford (SD) premises, was tasked with the 25 alone, and began accepting the buses there for store twelve days in advance of the conversion. The route was immediately in trouble, capacity loads and five-bus convoys characterising the first day with less than the full runout able to proceed further into the West End than Holborn Circus. Insult to injury came in that the 25's loss by First released the buses it would need to convert the 7 from RML to OPO the following week. There were four double-deckers on the 25 on 29 June, but these Tridents delivered for the 8 were just strike day extras and as 'free' potentially as the 'MAs' due to not yet having been fitted with ticket machines. London General also made good use of its artics on the two strike days, adding several Waterloo-based examples to a Southfields-Victoria rail replacement which was kept going. Meanwhile, despite the operator and format change, the three ESQs with First continued, as this was operated on a separate

Route 25 is getting better from every angle

From Saturday 26 June 2004 new Bendy Buses will be on route 25

24 hour service

Oxford Circus – Bank – Stratford – Ilford

MAYOR OF LONDON   Transport for London

contract; they were transferred to the RV1 in September.

First placed its own second order for artics during June; 27 more Citaros for the 207, though still with no date specified for this much-postponed artic conversion, as the proposed site at North Acton was being protested by residents.

MA 30 was displayed at North Weald bus rally on 27 June; it spent time during the month with Cubic Transportation Systems Ltd of Redhill for software trials with the Oyster card validators fitted at all three doorways. Burnt stablemate MA 40 had been taken back to Germany and had a new rear fitted. One of the 73's other intended artics, MA 35, was loaned to the TRRL test centre in Crowthorne to ascertain what kind of effect speed humps would have – while damaging to the chassis of buses and cars alike while actually increasing pollution on the spot due to vehicles revving up again after they'd slowed down to negotiate them, these 'sleeping policemen' had become a widespread scourge in the last decade and a half. In latter years they'd been modified so that buses' wheels could pass between the raised sections which were otherwise still too wide for cars to cross without slowing down. Still another, MA 39, spent late July and August with Arriva Merseyside to see if routes into Liverpool were any more, or less, appropriate for artics than in London.

Above: **Providing maximum antagonism at North Weald on 27 June 2004, MA 30 (BX04 MYY) from the batch intended to take over the 73! A little confusion had arisen over which of Arriva's new MAs was the one burnt out on its way from Germany, Mercedes-Benz having succeeded in concealing its identity from the wider world but in the process frustrating the record-keepers among us even more than they'd been doing already. When MA 30 appeared at North Weald, belief that this had been the lost one was resolved; it turned out to have been MA 40 instead. The 'AR' code is hopeful, but Tottenham, despite its expensive rebuilding that increased its floor plan, wouldn't be able to accommodate them and the 73 had to be reallocated to Lea Valley.** *Author*

Left: **The controversial 'better from every angle' leaflet, in this first version of two featuring the generic bendy bus based on the photograph of Arriva MA 30 at North Weald and thus incorrectly mimicking the blue-skirted Stagecoach East London ones on the 25.**

Oyster was now gearing up for universal adoption, the Pre-Pay variant being phased in during June. To impress this on passengers, Stagecoach Selkent's 23002 was treated during June to an all-over ad in the sky blue colour synonymous with the Oyster card, complete with curved dark-blue skirt set off by a white line and lettering above the windows declaring that the cost of Oyster Pre-Pay journeys was just 70p. It returned to red in October, and a darker shade thereof; the treatment included a white roof, the distinctly unsatisfactory non-solution to the problem of overheating of buses encountered during every summer. The instruction to TfL contractors that every new contract from 1 July 2004 be commenced with buses in a greater proportion of red than even hitherto put an end to the likelihood of liveries more ornate than skirts, though even those would be outlawed in the end. First never bothered with any accoutrements whatsoever and Arriva's subsequent deliveries would only have the yellow tape; the body design with its excess glass precluded anything more, like the 'cow horns' of its other buses.

They called 3 September 2004 Black Friday – the day on which 100 Routemasters were taken out of service on three routes, the 9, 390 and 73 in chronological order of last bus in. The following day saw the 73 set going again with its new Citaros, MA 30-76; as usual, the existing garage, Tottenham, could not accommodate them despite improvements to the site which had doubled its capacity only four years earlier, so it was reallocated to Lea Valley (LV), a new open-field site commissioned at the start of 2004 and fitted-out during the summer with a workshop and vehicle hoists (though no canteen accommodation; meal breaks were taken at Tottenham). As it happened, this base was within sight of Edmonton (EC), but separated from it by the River Lee Navigation. As Arriva London North's capacity requirements fluctuated over subsequent years contingent on its tendering successes or defeats, both of these scratch garages would have more to say in the history of artics in London. The 73's PVR had been boosted in the interim to 42, but this was still not enough to forestall heavy overcrowding from the outset, which was exacerbated by the inevitable bunching. Its rather useful in-service garage projections beyond Stoke Newington to Tottenham Swan were cut back to Seven Sisters, a geographical compromise between the two normal stands, neither of which could take artics. This also allowed dead journeys to reach Lee Valley via Tottenham Hale without having to turn around. Despite the long odds, Arriva London North's newest artic operation managed to escape the worst attentions of the tabloids, who were in position to observe from the first Monday peak (reported on for the *Evening Standard* by this author) and settled down, though one particular blogger living along Upper Street in Islington was driven damn near to suicide over the coming months by the sheer impossibility of getting a seat any more. An official leaflet with a graphic of the concertina between halves of a bendy was issued at this point with the strapline 'Route 73 is getting better from every angle'. Since it wasn't, a lawsuit was actually initiated which at least got TfL to alter the 'getting better' expression to plain 'changing'.

Right: **The second 'better from every angle' leaflet made its debut with the 73's one-manning, introducing the bellows close-up.**

London Buses

Route 73
is getting better from every angle

From Saturday 4 September 2004 new bendy buses will be on Route 73.

Victoria – King's Cross – Stoke Newington/Seven Sisters

MAYOR OF LONDON   Transport for London

Due to the late delivery of MA 40 following its post-fire rebuild (it eventually arrived in October), a demonstrator was taken on loan from Evobus. Numbered MD 1 (rather than being another MA due to having a different radio system), it was registered BX54 EBC and was in red livery with a yellow skirt. After coming off loan in October. would go on to see service with two further London artic operators and end up with the second of them permanently, but for the moment all that singled it out, apart from its livery, was its LED blind box set and standard Mercedes-Benz bus interior of most uninspiring grey moquette. The other unusual artic, Hispano-bodied Volvo B7LA X 62, was transferred from London General to Arriva London North during September and put into service

on the 149, lasting a month. Stagecoach 23004, cannibalised for parts during August, was restored to service in September.

London Central's artics for the 12, MALs 62-94 (representing an increase in the order from 32 to 33), were delivered to Evobus in Coventry during August and September. Five were taken for training at Camberwell but the rest were not brought to the capital till the week before the conversion on 6 November. As its Routemasters departed in a blaze of Fireworks Night-inspired glory the evening before, they were taken to Go-Ahead's own storage site at Mandela Way (which would, in the fullness of time, became a garage of its own and one that would operate artics) and swapped for MALs. The simultaneous conversion of the night service (renumbered from N12 earlier in the year) from AVL/PVL operation to MAL meant that the first journeys with artics were operated before the last RMLs had come out of service! MALs 62-94 operated, as did the previous RMs and RMLs, out of Camberwell and for a change requiring no garage reallocations. The termini were rejigged so that buses stood in Cavendish Square at the Oxford Circus end of the route, and at Friern Road rather than Etherow Street at the Dulwich end. To take on the 12's roads west of Oxford Circus, the 390, one-manned two months previously, was extended from Marble Arch to Notting Hill Gate. MA 94 was the last to arrive, and until it did, MD 1 of yellow skirt fame was taken on loan.

The 207 was also pencilled in for artic conversion on this date, but had it postponed again to January 2005, then to February and then indefinitely as the move to set up a base at North Acton collapsed. The numbers chosen for its 27-strong order, which were

Above: **The Hispano-bodied Volvo B7LA X 62 (FJ53 LZX) spent part of September 2004 on the 149; neither this nor the Scania with Arriva London North distinguished themselves, various niggles combining to curtail their loan spells and not persuading any artic operators to try out chassis other than the Citaro. Here it is at Stoke Newington.** *Steve Maskell*

Left: **Talk about treason and plot, and since it was in Peckham, undoubtedly no small amount of gunpowder as well! The last day of crew operation on the 12 was Friday 5 November 2004, and the final pair were Contract Services' RM 9 and RML 2725; the former (VLT 9) is seen at the end, about to set off on the last journey from Dulwich Library.** *Author*

Right: Go-Ahead's third batch of MAs (or third and a half if you count the three replacements for the burnt ones) comprised MALs 62-94 and for once, they fitted inside their operating garage, Camberwell, without the need for any routes to move out. The western portion was sheared off to add to the 390, rendering the 12's new permanent terminus Oxford Circus, albeit at a new stand at Margaret Street due to lack of room caused by so many other routes being curtailed there. On 27 November MAL 87 (BX54 UDU) is seen on stand. *Author*

Right: Trafalgar Square was substantially revamped at the end of 2002 to turn the square into a pedestrian plaza. This squeezed cars and buses onto a roundabout that unfortunately produced instant and massive tailbacks from all directions. For the purposes of this book, Trafalgar Square would come to be a hub for three of the artic routes, and on 3 July 2005 Camberwell's MAL 69 (BX54 UCT) is seen pulling up alongside two K6 telephone boxes. *Author*

already in the process of delivery to Evobus at Coventry by November 2004, skipped six allocated to First artics in Dublin to span EA 11039-11065. It had taken over a year since the grand First London renumbering for ECA 30xx fleetnumbers to be physically changed to EA 110xx on Westbourne Park's contingent. A deal was struck with Arriva to store them at Tottenham Marshes until the route was converted, the latest date by year's end being settled on as May.

On 18 November a third articulated chassis model made its appearance; YN54 ALO, a Scania OmniCity CN94UA of AB48T+89 capacity. Arriva London North took it for evaluation and numbered it OM 1, sending it out over the 73 and, ominously, the 38 roads on 26 November, and then putting it into service on 30 November, though fitfully due to problems with its plug doors. It was different in that both ends were the same length rather than the long front/short rear of the

Citaro, but the associated manoeuvrability problems were not insurmountable; still, not enough to prompt any orders for any. Like X 62 and MD 1, OM 1 too would rove around the operators; X 62 turned up with Stagecoach East London on 25 November and was used on the 25 from 6-9 December; it was supposed to last another week but broke down. The highest-numbered two of Waterden Road's fleet, 23076 and 23077, were fitted with tachographs for private-hire work, becoming the first artic re-registrations when they received WLT 886 and VLT 240 respectively. 23002 lost its Oyster card livery in October and OM 1 was returned to Scania on 18 December.

CHAPTER SIX

2005

On 15 January both the 453 and its progenitor, the 53, had their peak-hour frequencies reduced from every six minutes to every 7.5 minutes. This was a brave move to address capacity problems suffered on the 25, and accordingly Citaros 23031-23035 were transferred from Plumstead to Waterden Road to boost the route's PVR by five to 42. That also removed the need for the temporary parking area at North Greenwich. The 453's PVR was now 25.

Despite a downturn in opinion of artics in London, two more routes were proposed for conversion in 2005, and like the 73 and 12, the 29 and 38 were about the very worst choices. The 38 was now the route with the biggest Routemaster PVR and the 29, no matter how many buses were thrown at it, ate them up and begged for more. The decision was particularly irresponsible in the case of the 29 when it was already recognised how bad

congestion problems were across Camden, where the overlapping structure of the route ensured that getting a seat northbound was impossible unless one made one's way to the beginning of the northern overlap there. In fact bets were hedged by offering two options; one in which the 29 would be converted to artic, but lose its Wood Green-Palmers Green section to an extension of the 141. A second option would leave the 29 as it was, but section off the northern end as 429. In either case the 29 would lose its service north of Wood Green and the 21 would be extended from Moorgate to Newington Green to help the 141, whose potential passengers into the City didn't stand a chance if they attempted to board south of Newington Green. The first option was chosen, its tender under Tranche 204 awarded to and retained by Arriva London North in April for implementation in January 2006.

Right: **There did exist some sense of planning and rejigging when conditions didn't match timetabled requirements, regardless of the rigidity of contracts, and such a recasting on 15 January 2005 added desperately-needed reinforcements to the 25. This was accomplished by giving it five of the 453's artics, one of which is 23035 (LX03 HEV), seen in Regent Street on 27 November 2004. Disregard the blinds; it's only 2.45 pm and the N453 won't come on for another ten hours!**
Author

With this in mind, as well as the need to house the buses transferred to Arriva London North following the closure of Arriva East Herts & Essex's Debden depot, the 149 (day and night services alike) was reallocated from Edmonton to Lea Valley with MA 1-29 on 19 February, this allowing an extra bus to be added to the 73 to make its PVR 43.

On 12 February Scania CN94UA YN54 ALO came back to town for trials over the 18 with First, commencing on 15 March but operating sporadically until mid-April due to continued problems with its doors. The Hispano-bodied Volvo B7LA was meant

to accompany it but took up service with Lothian in Edinburgh instead. YN54 ALO did put in an appearance at Cobham open day on 3 April when it satisfied the legal requirement for at least one low-floor bus alongside the classics to transport the less able-bodied to and fro.

The 207's conversion, set as 14 May 2005, was put forward to 9 April now that a new base had been found. It was in Rigby Lane in Hayes and was coded variously HZ (TfL) or HS (First). Acton Tram Depot and Uxbridge withdrew, and the new 427 took on the former TNLs to allow the main route

Above: **Scania's '4' series offered a common look whether single-deck, double-deck or articulated, and the end result was attractive. CN94UA artic YN54 ALO was evaluated by three of the operators, and in April 2005 is seen at Sudbury on the 18 under the control of a Willesden Junction driver from First London.** *Haydn Davies*

Left: **On 19 February 2005 the need to fill Edmonton with the TfL buses displaced by the closure of Debden forced the ejection of the 149 and its MAs to Lea Valley, where it could now bunk up with the 73 and share its fleet. Accordingly, one of the 73's original motors, MA 50 (BX04 MYU) is seen on the 149 on 5 March, at which point Edmonton Green bus station as we knew it was under comprehensive reconstruction that obliged the 149 to vacate it for the moment and lay over elsewhere.** *Peter Horrex*

Above: **The 207's second and this time permanent tenure with artics commenced on 9 April 2005, EA 11039-11065 taking over from the TNLs on a shortened route operating the eastern two-thirds of the complete route. Operating from new premises at Hayes is EA 11065 (LK05 FCC), seen heading east when new; the balance was renumbered 427 and retained Tridents like TNL 32915 (W915 VLN), while the express 607 continued as before.** *Haydn Davies*

Below: **One of the 18's original vehicles, EA 11025 (LK53 FCD), visits the 207 at Shepherd's Bush on 17 April 2005; both batches carried a common set of blinds and could thus be made best use of when going to and from Willesden Junction for maintenance.** *Author*

to fall back to Hayes By-Pass. Although new at the end of 2004, all but the first two of EA 11039-11065 were registered with 05-plates, 11039 and 11040 being licensed in February with 54-registrations so that they could train drivers. In spite of the 207's conversion to artic, the night counterpart remained double-deck due to its covering not only the former extent out to Uxbridge, but substantial portions of central London as well on its way from Holborn to line of route. Arriva's Tottenham Marshes site was thus not needed any more, and closed after 31 March after expiry of the lease; in the interim a yard near Hackney was used. Maintenance for the 207's EAs was the responsibility of Willesden Junction garage, which was expanded during the year after planning permission was granted on 17 March. This meant that buses from Willesden Junction and Hayes would turn out on each other's routes, blinds being carried for both the 18 and 207. A little difficulty was encountered with fuel-tank contamination at Hayes left behind by the previous tenant, resulting in refuelling from the Shepherd's Bush end of the 207 having to be accomplished by a trip to and from Willesden Junction out of service, but this was sorted out pretty quickly.

Another fire scare ensued when on 12 March MAL 39's rear caught fire at New Cross Gate while as NX301 on the 436; the media were all over it, but without any knowledge as to the cause other than speculation. After it was towed to Evobus's Southall premises, MD 1 came back for a second spell during March and April. MAL 40 was also treated at Southall following damage sustained on or around 8 April; it was back by 3 May.

Above and below left: **It seemed that the 436 couldn't get a break; two more of its MALs were incapacitated in the late winter and early spring of 2005 and thus MD 1 (BX54 EBC) was borrowed again. Here it is at Vauxhall on 3 May 2005 (front offside view) and on 21 April (rear offside view).** Both: *Author*

Below: **The simple seat moquette offered on base-specification Citaros and accordingly carried by MD 1.**

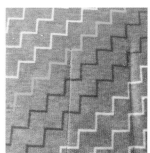

Left: **The lifecycle of all-over adverts in London might be compared to eating chocolate cake; after glutting themselves during the 1970s, London Transport got sick of them and it wasn't for another twenty years that TfL placed advertising revenue above aesthetics and had another try at the concept. Artics don't necessarily lend themselves to all-over ads unless a special effort is made, and this scheme for the University of East London on 23034 (LX03 HEU) didn't really imprint itself until the front was painted orange too. This bus, seen at Aldgate on 28 April 2006, was one of the five transferred from Plumstead to Waterden Road in January.** *Richard Godfrey*

Below left: **The second UEL all-over ad was on 23033 (LX03 HEJ), another January reinforcement to the 25, and was blue-based all over. While both ads lasted three years, that on 23033 was amended mid-term; the earlier version, seen here as the bus lays over at Holles Street on 25 June 2005, was less exciting. A stroke of luck has brought both University of East London ads into Oxford Street together.** *Richard Godfrey*

Bottom left: **23031 (LX03 HBY) was transferred to Waterden Road on 15 January 2005 and in June was treated to an advert for Tower Hamlets council in concert with a drive to improve air quality. The 25 ran past Victoria Park, the theme of the graphic, though hopefully not too many people walked or cycled into the bus, thinking its realistic photographic representation to be the real thing! It is seen leaving Stratford in August.** *Graham Smith*

Two Stagecoach East London Citaros donned all-over advert liveries during March on behalf of the University of East London (formerly East London Poly); 23033 was in light blue and 23034 was in orange, though until the end of April 23034's front remained in fleet livery. 23033's livery was further modified with more colourful graphics.

The date was now set for the conversion of the 38 – 29 October 2005 – and Arriva combined the orders for both this and the 29 so that the 38's forty-six MAs would be followed by another thirty-five for the 29, incorporating two added to the 38. These would carry blinds for both routes, and started delivery to Coventry in June. The Tottenham Marshes site was leased for a second spell; while the Citaros were awaited, it held Original London Sightseeing Tour vehicles not needed during the winter and then accommodated Leaside Travel's fleet ejected from Edmonton by the reconstruction of that location. MAs 77-122, intended for the 38, started appearing in the capital from July, dispatched to storage at Lea Valley and gradually readied for training.

Stagecoach East London now took OM 1 on loan, displaying it at the Waterden Road open day on 25 June and putting it into service on the 25 four days later; it lasted until 12 July. The standees in Lea Valley's MA 48 could at least rely on some entertainment while they swayed, as in June Crystal Eyes screens were fitted in both sections. When they worked, they played advertisement-based film strips. These were also fitted to New Cross's allocation on the 436 during the summer, the work being carried out at Walworth. Entertainment was also the point of putting Go-Ahead MALs on the Epsom racecourse service from Morden on Derby Day, 3 and 4 June. Waterden Road's 23031 was given an all-over advert (omitting the front) in July for Tower Hamlets Council, the graphic being of Victoria Park with 'Air quality – what does it mean to you?' admonition above.

Below: **Scania CN94UA demonstrator OM 1 (YN54 ALO) had one last try along a London artic corridor in 2005, operating from Stagecoach East London's Waterden Road on the 25 between 29 June and 12 July, but it was too late for Scania or Volvo really to wean the established operators off their Citaros, even with all their problems. On 4 July it is seen at Holborn performing as WA43 and carrying some very simple blinds in the rather thick New Johnston Bold typeface. The considerable difference in the proportions of the front and rear assembly as compared to the Citaro G are evident.** *Richard Godfrey*

The urgent need to cover for the Piccadilly Line following the terrorist bombing of 7 July 2005 prompted two artics from Lea Valley to be diverted from the 73 and 149 to provide peak-hour extras along the 29 between Wood Green and Finsbury Park from the 11th. On the 14th, MAs 77, 79 and 80, three of the artics in storage in preparation for the 38, were taken from storage at Lea Valley and replaced them in the same role, though without ticket machines. MA 85 and 88, delivered to Lea Valley on the 15th, joined them from the 17th until 3 August; all displayed '29' number blinds and 'Rail Replacement' via/ultimates. At least that got the 29 some practice in seeing what kind of loads it would carry (or which of them would chance to pay, ticket machines or no ticket machines!) following its conversion to artic, which was firmed up about this time as 14 January 2006. MAs 77-88 were licensed in August (with 05-plates, though mixed between BX- and BU-marks) to permit driver training, which was undertaken from Tottenham Marshes; the rest were 55-reg.

If the open-boarding format of artics was one cause of a fall in fares revenue (and perhaps countered by a hefty increase in the already eye-watering £5 of the Congestion Charge to £8 from 4 July 2005), another one was about to be undertaken; the equally

Left: **On 19 June 2004 the new stand at Waterloo was brought into use, hacked out of the widest section of the approach to the former Bull Ring roundabout now taken up by the IMAX cinema. While primarily a place for 139s and 243s to stand, it was also a good photographic pitch in late afternoon to catch 521s coming out of their own stand, as with Red Arrow MAL 12 (BX02 YYT) on 7 June. New blind sets are now in Waterloo MALs, but unfortunately and inexplicably, the word 'Station' has been omitted, leading people to think the 521 terminates on the bridge itself rather than the railhead some few hundred yards beyond it; worse was to come in terms of standards of information.** *Author*

irresponsible introduction of free travel for under-16s from 1 September 2005. While cashless operation was still expected to be rolled out in 2006, a survey of articulated routes reported a 6.3% fare evasion rate, which was about on a par with normal routes, though again it must be emphasised that these were only the ones actually caught dodging their fare.

Notting Hill Carnival had for some years seen a 12X operated with RMLs spare from the 12; now that they had all gone, this role was switched to a seasonal augmentation of the 436 known as 436X and operated with twelve MALs from Waterloo.

As the 38's conversion to bendy bus loomed, the old problem of accommodation reared its ugly head, and not for the last time, even though no further routes were tendered on the basis of artics after the 29. Once again, as with six of the twelve routes that would come to operate artics, an alternative garage had to be used for the 38. In this case, there was a perfect site sitting underused and underappreciated only half a mile from line of route – Ash Grove, currently shared by East Thames Buses and Hackney Community Transport, none of whose routes operated even close to the site. While HCT was allowed to remain, a sidestep of the normal tendering

Left: **When such large numbers flock from all over London to cram into the ever-smaller confines permitted to hold the Notting Hill Carnival, extra buses have to be put on, and now that Routemasters' traditional route 12X was no longer an option, an augmentation was added to the 436 instead, guest-starring Waterloo MALs. Here at Notting Hill Gate as Carnival winds down on Sunday 28 August 2005 is MAL 19 (BX02 YZC).** *Author*

process was thus undertaken for the routes of East Thames whereby the 128 and 150 were offered out. This was implemented on 15 October, the 128 going to Arriva London North (the Barking premises commenced by Grey-Green) and the 150 to First; in compensation, the 1 was handed over to East Thames Buses out of a new 80-capacity depot in Mandela Way adjacent to Go-Ahead's premises there. This base also took East Thames's existing single-deck services, the 42 and 393.

The conversion of the 38 was particularly bitterly received, especially when accompanied by the 'changing from every angle' service leaflet handed out at Victoria on the ceremonial last Routemaster day. After the exit of Clapton's Routemaster fleet on the night of 28/29

October, it meant that there were now just two Routemaster routes left, and while only three routes were directly converted from Routemaster to bendy bus (the 73, 12 and 38), it was not difficult for many to blame the artics for the withdrawal of the RM. The 38 operated in a similarly confused manner to the 149 when it started with artics; while the buses were predominantly housed at Ash Grove (coded 'AE' rather than its traditional 'AG'), their drivers signed on at Clapton and the artics took on 'CT' codes. Evobus established a facility there for maintenance, but it was envisaged that the garage be mothballed and its routes transferred out. The N38 remained double-deck, with DLAs from the daytime 242 and VLWs from the 253.

Once the 38's MAs had replaced its RMLs, the final batch started arriving at Tottenham Marshes during November, comprising MAs 125-157. At this point Arriva London North started getting in on the re-registration act, using ex-Routemaster marks from doomed Leaside Travel coaches to spiff up two MAs with reasonably matching fleetnumbers; thus MA 5 donned 205 CLT and MA 85 185 CLT. There would be fourteen such from Arriva and three Stagecoach.

Attrition in London's traffic-choked streets caused accidents of one kind or another to MAs 13, 53 and 68 during the autumn, the latter two colliding with each other on 31 October. Repair work was outsourced to a myriad of concerns, MA 68 being done in-house at Enfield while MA 53 was sent to Caetano at Waterlooville and MA 13 to Unitec at Thurrock. MA 148 was late arriving due to a mishap on delivery resulting in

it having to be sent back to Germany. But whether the humble Londoner liked the buses or not, perhaps someone higher placed expressed their displeasure in August when Plumstead's 23025 was struck by lightning outside its home garage!

Perhaps to commemorate their victory over Routemasters, in December, the same month as the last RMs and RMLs made their spectacular exit from frontline service, eleven more Arriva MAs were re-registered with RM marks. MA 17, 19, 24, 30, 61, 70, 80, 93, 98, 119 and 124 gained 217/519/324/330/361 CLT, 70/480/593/398/319/124 CLT. Most of these came off the coaches made spare with the dissolution of Leaside Travel, enough being spare to similarly re-register three VLWs. Prior to the 29's conversion, ten of its incoming MAs were plucked from store to join a dozen of the 38's examples mounting a rail replacement over the Jubilee Line between 27-30 December. Three of them, MAs 133, 134 and 136, were diverted to Ash Grove to help out on the 38, though MA 136 was damaged in a rear-end collision while doing so and was sent to Unitec for repair. The Jubilee Line rail job also saw help from London Central MALs.

It was grist to the media mill when a Stagecoach driver was crushed to death between two artics at Greenwich on 21 December; 23024 was taken to a police compound in Charlton as subject of the subsequent investigation, which determined that the handbrake had not been applied on the second artic that had arrived to help the first's driver with a tail light problem. Waterden Road's 23032 was loaned to Plumstead over Christmas to fill in.

Above: **Registration 217 CLT, new on Routemaster RM 1217, spent 1991-2003 on Olympian L 217 and 2003-2005 on a Leaside Travel coach known as DPL 1. In December it was attached to MA 17 (ex-BX04 MXR) and the result is seen at Marble Arch on 23 July 2009. Inevitably, fashions would change again and in May 2009 MA 17 gained back its original mark (shrewdly held onto; see page 74) so that Enviro400 T 17 could take on 217 CLT.** *Author*

CHAPTER SEVEN

2006

Below: **Artics shoulder the blame for the withdrawal of Routemasters, but it's only partially true, with just three routes out of the twelve converted directly. Still, the bitter enemies can be compared as they pause at the lights approaching Trafalgar Square on 8 December 2005, the penultimate day of RMs and RMLs in normal service. On the left, testing out the 29 road shortly after delivery, is Arriva London North MA 129 (BX55 FWN), the German upstart, beside its all-British counterpart, RM 346 (SVS 615, ex-346 CLT); two vastly different forms of public transport, and at the time of writing, both now gone.** *Author*

The final artic conversion took place on 14 January 2006, and the 29 was soon mired in media excoriation, the belief being that this extraordinarily busy and vitally important trunk service had degenerated rapidly into a criminals' paradise of fare-dodging and un-policed violence. It wasn't entirely inaccurate an appraisal, unfortunately. One thing that the 29's conversion did achieve was the final removal of all step-entrance double-deckers from frontline TfL work, the outgoing DLPs being sent to displace the last Ms from schools augmentation for Leaside Travel.

It was too much to ask for the MAs to turn in Wood Green garage's forecourt other than six journeys restricted to the off-peak and on Saturday and Sunday afternoons, so both the

29 and N29 were reallocated to Edmonton garage. The 29 was reconfigured to disgorge its passengers short of the station and then stand in Redvers Road, coming round to start again at a specially extended first stop. The N29, losing only its Enfield to Ponders End section, actually went over to MA first, due to the first night duty spending its first few hours from 20.45 as a 29; MA 146 as EC271 did the honours. With no further conversions planned, Arriva London North saw no further need for Tottenham Marshes and surrendered the lease on 31 January.

All the artics were now in service. Progress from here on was in the interests of maximising capacity and gradual improvement; for instance the new iBus programme of GPS-assisted vehicle location

Right: **The last artic conversion was that of the 29, the belief still being that the movement of masses of people took precedence over whether many of them would be able to sit down. This after so much effort and expenditure on low-floor buses, which in themselves removed up to a third of the seating capacity of previous generations. This shot of DLP 47 (Y547 UGC) departing Wood Green on 5 March 2005 illustrates a particular problem in that only well spread-out open-plan garages could admit artics, and not traditional closely-packed bases like Wood Green.** Author

Below right: **Like the 25, the 29 was the kind of trunk route that would soak up everything thrown at it and still beg for more, and like the 25, deteriorated commensurately post-double-deck. On 12 March 2006 MA 146 (BX55 FXK) passes Warren Street. Edmonton was now the operating garage, no room being found in Wood Green for the sixty-foot artics.** Author

software was about to take effect across London. This benefited the passenger in that a visual display was fitted to buses to show the current stop and incorporate the 'Bus Stopping' notice previously carried and illuminated when the bell was pressed. Where artics were concerned, the pair of iBus indicators was fitted in each section where double-deckers had one on each deck, and five Lea Valley MAs based on the 149 were the first to receive them, in January 2006.

When London Central's MAL 39 was returned to service at New Cross in January 2006 following protracted repair of its fire damage, MD 1 was transferred to Camberwell and took up on the 12 for three months. In February. Route 38-based MA 98, already distinguished with its 398 CLT vanity plate, was treated to an all-over advert (barring the front) for the 'China in London' promotion

Left: **For all the criticism of artics, even from this quarter, all the work necessary to prepare road and bus-stop infrastructure was carried out without too much difficulty. The best example along the 29 road is the southbound bay at Wood Green station, which was extended to accommodate one artic, and that's where MA 125 (BX55 FWJ), the first of this route's batch, is taking on passengers when captured during the afternoon of 21 January 2006.** Author

Above: **iBus quickly calmed down from being an annoying intrusion into the otherwise (ideally) noise-free aspect of bus travel, becoming a useful accessory that also facilitated the standardisation of bus-stop infrastructure with unique names for each stop. It wasn't until later that it was realised that iBus's true potential actually lay in the information behind it, but in the years before smartphones, the most important aspect was the visual indicators (on artics, one in each half). This is the fitment behind the cab of a route 73 MA.** *Jack Marian*

in time for the Chinese New Year, which in 2006 was that of the Dog (with no aspersions on Citaros' reputation!). MA 124 regained its original plate in April as RM 1124 had been selected as one of Arriva's Heritage fleet and it wouldn't do to see it going around with VYJ 806.

The five-year tendering cycle was about to come round again to the first artic routes, but since the 507 and 521 had first been offered and awarded a new aspect had been introduced whereby the contract was extended by two years for good performance; therefore in March, these routes' expiry, scheduled for June 2007, would not now occur until June 2009. This would be the only artic route to get

two more years, though the criteria would of course change.

One of the least welcome 'advancements' to bus accoutrements in the first decade of the 21st century was the dumbing down of blinds; after considerable resistance when this was first tried on a 2001 delivery of London Central PVLs, it was adopted in earnest during 2006. The reduction of information to just a destination was bewilderingly contemptuous of passengers' needs, especially since timetable information was simultaneously reduced to little more than an overview of routes' frequencies rather than the actual times themselves. It's hard to explain the rationale for such a patronising attitude towards passengers, but this was only the culmination of a long spell of declining standards. Where artics were concerned, the sophisticated nature of their smartblinds and the fact that most were route-bound made the introduction of single-line destinations later to appear than on other types. It had thus proven barely worth making the effort to provide extra physical blind-box space for the passenger if all TfL could be bothered subsequently to specify was a destination, additionally wasting acres of linen without via points. Not to mention, they just looked ugly. At least one side-effect was a move away from the overly-chubby New Johnston variety of the original London Transport font that had been used on artics' blinds from new.

A curious piece of spin celebrated the reconstruction of Edmonton garage by holding an official reopening ceremony on 23 May, whereby MA 157 was handed over as 'the last Citaro bendy bus'. Both garage and vehicle had been in service for some time but it made a good press occasion. Less positive for PR were the figures published by TfL in August that of the five routes to report the most Code Red calls by drivers, artic-operated routes 25, 29 and 207 came first, third and fifth.

On 23 June 2006 came the stunning news that Stagecoach had sold its East London and Selkent operations, which were bought by the Australian-based Macquarie Bank for £263.5 million. Collectively known as the East London Bus Group (ELBG) following the completion of the sale on 30 August, its two companies were branded as East London and Selkent, the sail barge and hops logos returning for each respectively and the numeric fleetnumbering system retained. All-over red was to be the new livery, completing the downward spiral aesthetically since Stagecoach had been obliged to delete its rear stripes; now the dark blue skirts too began to disappear. Waterden Road's 23044 was the first artic with East London fleetnames during August, 23021 simultaneously doing the honours for Selkent. Most of the group's artics had offside advert panels fitted, the panels chosen obscuring the position of the former Stagecoach fleetnames. When subsequently applied, new fleetnames were above the windows in the first bay behind the cab. Arriva London North's MAs gained advert frames next. On 1 August 23063 was re-registered 630 DYE; close enough!

The work ascertaining the cause of its fire done, MAL 51 was brought back from Surrey to London on the back of a low-loader on 10 August and deposited with a scrapyard in Willesden, which had broken it up by the end of the month.

Left: **In 2006 MA 98 (398 CLT, ex-BX55 FUV) of the 38's contingent received an all-over ad encouraging tourists to visit China. Not long after being re-registered with the plate originally belonging to Routemaster RM 1398, it heads down Charing Cross Road towards Victoria.** *Haydn Davies*

Right: **Stagecoach Selkent in turn became plain Selkent, bringing back the hops logo that had surmounted the fleetname from District days through to that of its pre-privatisation subsidiary identity. This is the result on artics, exemplified in Whitehall on 31 March 2007 by Plumstead's 23008 (LX03 HCG). Quite where the Mercedes-Benz three-pointed star badge from the front of the bus has gone is not known; if this had been 1987 rather than 2007 it would more than likely be on a gold chain round someone's neck!** *Author*

With much-postponed effect from Saturday 9 September, the 453's terminating arrangements were altered so that the route turned at Deptford Bridge at a purpose-built stand capable of accommodating two artics. TfL had rather missed a trick by not livening up the dead runs to Lewisham, which remained, as it has done since 1999, without a direct link to the West End. This allowed three buses to be taken off the 453's PVR and prompt the first inter-company transfers. As with the 25, the 18 had struggled with capacity issues and it was thus First that was the beneficiary

from 23 September. Five artics were added to Willesden Junction's fleet; former Selkent 23001-23004 became EA 11066-11069 and the fifth was former Arriva London North and London Central demonstrator BX54 EBC, which was slotted in at the chronological beginning of the EA class as EA 11000, losing its LED blinds at the same time to bring it into line. All five had their skirts repainted, EA 11000 initially gaining a black one before this too was painted red like the other four. This didn't stop Waterden Road from having to help out Plumstead with regular loans.

Below: **And here is the combination of ELBG-owned Selkent and all-red livery, seen in the person of 23015 (LX03 HCU) in Whitehall.** *Steve Maskell*

Left: **Despite East London and Selkent being separate trading names, which continued into the ELBG era, the operations had long been unified and loans to and from each outfit were not uncommon. The visit during November 2006 of University of East London-liveried 23033 (LX03 HEJ) to Plumstead and the 453 only eighteen months after its transfer to the 25 was an eye-opener, however, in that it took the advert perhaps out of geographical range of its catchment area. Unfortunately, the new set of simplified blinds brought in did not include the 453, leading to this awkward attempt when the bus was sighted at County Hall on the 6th, amid construction of the Park Plaza Hotel. Whoever fashioned the makeshift destination won't have been the first person completely foxed by the spelling of Marylebone relative to its pronunciation!** *Author*

Left: **23034 (LX03 HEU) was also apt to be loaned across the river to Plumstead; this was an every-weekend occurrence at one point, but an old set of blinds had to be cut up and carried in the windscreen, as seen at the Elephant & Castle one sunny afternoon.** *Haydn Davies*

Left: **By the time this shot of 23033 (LX03 HEJ) was taken in Parliament Square in September 2007, a bit more effort had been made with the blinds, a set of inserts having been run up to carry in the windscreen. For all the relief powerblinds gave drivers, they were not easily replaced or updated, and the limited nature of artic operations didn't make it worth the while to print more sets for loans like these.** *Haydn Davies*

Right: **The activation of the 453's long-intended stand at Deptford Bridge removed the need for the route to run dead to Lewisham to turn, freeing up four artics to be deployed elsewhere. The 18 was identified as the route in most need of a boost, and accordingly, via a trip to lessors Dawson Rentals, 23001-23004 became First EA 11066-11069. The lowest-numbered of this quartet, EA 11066 (LV52 VFW) is captured approaching Euston on 10 November 2008 without the 'EA' part of its new fleetnumber applied. It was not unknown for these buses to switch to and from the 207 if necessary, the allocations at Hayes and Willesden Junction forming something more akin to a pool than allocations from most other garages.**
Martin Clitheroe

Below: **The fifth addition to the 18's roster at Willesden Junction was the former demonstrator BX54 EBC, which was numbered EA 11000 and had its blind box modified to accept rollers to TfL standard. Its yellow skirt has been repainted black, but that affectation would itself disappear in due course.**
Haydn Davies

On 28 October a new stand came into use at the Clapton end of the 38, carved out of the Kenninghall Roundabout and with capacity for more artics than had the spot underneath the willow tree beside Clapton Pond. Where Clapton garage was concerned, this former route 38 base had duly been emptied on 1 April with the transfer of the 242 and 253 to Stamford Hill, despite continuing to serve as the on-paper allocation of the buses physically domiciled at Ash Grove. While also still serving as an engineering outpost of Evobus, on 1 December 2006 it was leased to the Siemens group, who were contracted to install iBus across all TfL contractors' fleets. Norwood would serve as the south-of-the-river centre for this work. Where the passenger impact of iBus was concerned, it took a long period of tinkering before the accompanying audio announcements were reduced from irritatingly frequent and overly loud to discreet background noise to accompany the usual hubbub expected inside bus saloons, but iBus had a future full of promise and was quickly implemented during 2007 and 2008.

The 507 and 521 having come up for tender again and been extended for two years, it was now the turn of the 436 and 453 and their night counterparts to go out again from December 2006 for implementation at the start of 2008.

On 18 December at 7 pm a Camberwell MAL on the 12 struck and killed a twelve-year-old girl in East Dulwich Road, Peckham Rye, while on New Year's Day New Cross's MAL 47 on the 436 swerved on Vauxhall Bridge and hit two female pedestrians, one of whom died; both MALs were inspected afterwards by the police as part of the inquest and Camberwell's MAL 84 was loaned to New Cross to cover.

CHAPTER EIGHT

2007

On 5 January the 25 formally introduced Friday- and Saturday-night short journeys from Oxford Circus to Stratford; these had been operated between 1-31 December but were successful enough to be made permanent. The night service was strengthened throughout on 30 June, becoming every 12 minutes (requiring 13 buses) and every ten at weekends (requiring 15).

East London's 23031 lost its Victoria Park advert in January 2007. Nos 23048 and 23066 were the first two ELBG Citaros otherwise to be repainted. 23010, 23016, 23031, 23036 and 23037 were repainted in March and 23047 in May.

Try as they might, TfL could not rake in enough revenue from buses to make them pay for themselves, especially with cock-eyed schemes like granting Income Support recipients half-price travel and entreating the hardly stable Venezuelan government to provide cut-price fuel; the only option was to continue to gouge motorists at the border, and to this end the Congestion Charging zone was extended westwards on 19 February 2007. A week earlier, the experimental service of the fuel-cell ESQs on the RV1 ended; while reasonably successful and another notch to the otherwise satisfactory reputation of the Citaro, the cost has precluded serious ventures in that direction ever since.

Below: **The sheer physical bulk that artics take up makes photographing them a challenge in itself; the purist will surely overlook the pedestrians that have otherwise got themselves right in the way of a clear nearside of MA 149 (BX55 FXO) as it bends the corner from Camden Road into Bayham Street on 8 July 2007.**
Peter Horrex

On 31 March the 507 and 521 gained an evening service, now coming off at 00.30 hours rather than between seven and eight PM; all route 521 shorts from Waterloo to St Paul's were projected through to London Bridge Station and the route was permitted to run northbound through the Kingsway underpass off-peak rather than circumnavigating Aldwych at those hours.

May 2007 brought an interesting fillip to an otherwise very quiet and stable year: the first artic contract change. While the 436 was retained by London Central with its existing MALs, the 453 was awarded to London General with a PVR of 23, increased by one.

It didn't look like meaning a great deal in mid-2007, but one Boris Johnson, Conservative MP for Henley-on-Thames,

Above: **Construction of the Olympic Park obliged not just East London's Waterden Road to up sticks, but First London's Stratford as well. The 25 was thus reallocated on 29 December to Rainham, some distance from the route's easternmost penetrations to Ilford (the Becontree Heath and Dagenham Works projections the route used to feature would have come in handy here). Thus it's going to be a long journey for 23077 (VLT 240, ex-LX04 LCW) as it pulls out of its Oxford Circus stand on 24 May 2008. As it turned out, Rainham was soon vacated in turn and the 25 moved into a much more appropriate encampment at the new, ultra-modern West Ham garage.** *Author*

stated his intention to run for Mayor in 2008; among his noted (and colourfully expressed) dislikes were bendy buses. With West London Transit officially shelved during August, the gravy train that had propelled Ken Livingstone's TfL had come to a halt, and popular opinion was shifting away from him, not least because of his perceived duplicity regarding the withdrawal of Routemasters. On the positive side, the win of the 2012 Olympics assured that a long-downtrodden swathe of East London would be revitalised in the run-up to the Games; however, the payoff was that the Stadium and its fellow buildings would obliterate three garages, one of which was East London's Waterden Road. ELBG had already made moves towards securing new premises by purchasing from Ensign the Ferry Lane depot in Rainham that had been vacated recently by First following the reconstruction of Dagenham, not to mention securing the former Post Office depot at West Ham for redevelopment into a large-capacity new garage, but time was of the essence.

East London 23063 was fitted in July with a rear advert panel that scrolled through three different adverts. 23033's University of East London advert was modified to a white base with more colourful graphics, though still with the blue front. It was apt to spend weekends on loan to Plumstead for the 453, undoubtedly broadening the potential student base to across the river. Unusual deployments this summer were of MAL 22 on park & ride duties at the Hampton Court Flower Show on 4 July, while the 436X of Notting Hill Carnival fame was again carried out with MALs.

Boris Johnson was now formally proposed as Conservative candidate for the Mayoral post and was chosen as such in September. For our purposes, not only was one of his ambitions to get rid of bendy buses, but another was to design a modern version of the Routemaster – if he was elected, perhaps a reversal of the incumbent's more unpopular policies could be accomplished! For the moment two more contract extensions were announced, those of the 149 and 18, prolonging their careers with bendies into 2010.

Although the 'traditional' fire problems of Citaros had been solved, that didn't help East London 23038, which, while on its way to Ilford to take up service on the 25 on 29 September, caught fire on the slip road to the A406 near Redbridge; the rear section was damaged. This time a heater unit was the cause and the vehicle was repairable. MA 122 suffered frontal damage when in collision with a coach in Piccadilly while operating on the 38 on 24 August, and rather more seriously, on 9 October a man became trapped under the wheels of 23054 after falling when he'd stepped off at the Clements Lane stop in Ilford and was dragged to his death for a mile in the direction of Manor Park.

In September London General ordered twenty-five new artics for the takeup of the 453, and like the rest they were Citaros. The design had undergone a spot of revision since the 29's intake eighteen months ago, the front and rear having been softened and the shape of the indicators changed; that was about all that could be done with such a basic rectangle of a design. The effect wasn't unbecoming on a bus that was already decent-looking by British standards; perhaps it was a relief that German designers were invariably as conservative as their British counterparts! A new garage was needed, naturally, and this was achieved ahead of time by activating Mandela Way, London General's storage and works site, as an operational garage from 3 November with the input of the 133.

Demolition work on the Olympic Park site was slated to start in January, with all occupied sites and businesses ordered to be vacated by 31 December 2005, and Waterden Road duly closed on the 29th, along with fellow East London garage Stratford and First's Hackney. The 25, by now the only route at Waterden Road since the move of the 15H's Routemasters into Bow on 22 September, was reallocated with its fleet to Rainham. It needed augmentation on two Sundays in October to cover for a Victoria Line closure, plus all four Sundays leading up to Christmas; all these were short journeys between Stratford and Aldgate. 23076 lost its WLT 886 mark in November and 23063 lost its scrolling rear advert by year's end.

Below: **MA 73 (BX04 NDK) approaches Edmonton Green on 16 July 2007. This unlovely but unforgettable terminus, with its concrete bridge and straight-through aspect, was revamped by 2007 as a bus station to TfL's latterly standard U-shaped configuration, which unfortunately ruled it out as a good photo pitch; thankfully angles remained at the roundabout and the stop to the south.** *Peter Horrex*

CHAPTER NINE

2008

The year began with New Cross's MALs on the 436 taking up another standard five-year contract term with effect from 9 February. iBus fitment, spreading rapidly on a garage-by-garage basis, was completed with Arriva London North by March. Where London Central and London General were concerned, a team was sent to the vehicles' home garages with the equipment rather than them calling in at Clapton or Norwood. This encompassed the allocations at New Cross and then Camberwell in April, with Waterloo treated in May as the first of London General's fleet. First's EAs were all done by May and East London brought up the rear, Siemens' mobile team fitting the 25's allocation within Rainham at the beginning of 2009.

On the 16th came the first and only change of operator for an artic route; the 453's Selkent Citaros stepped down and in came London General MAL 95-119, operating out of Mandela Way depot. MALs 2, 4, 24 and 31 had to be borrowed from Waterloo until all of the new buses were ready. As Selkent's were leased from Dawson Rentals, they were potentially available for fellow TfL contractors to lease in their own right to fill enhanced schedules where they were needed – and they were, either the articulated format proving too popular (perhaps due to the 'free bus' aspect ...) or the vehicles could plainly not accommodate enough seated passengers. Four of them (23027-23030) were immediately despatched as reinforcements to Rainham. The new MALs, to Euro 5 emissions

Below: **The only transfer of an artic-operated route from one company to another was that of the 453, which on 16 February 2008 passed to London General with MALs from Mandela Way. Here we got to see the subtle alterations to the Citaro's front as demonstrated at the bottom of Regent Street by MAL 115 (BP57 UYG); the indicators point up rather than down and the 'grille' is somewhat softened.** *Author*

specification, displayed new front and rear designs of a fairly discreet nature; their seats (only 47 of them this time as opposed to the usual 49, permitting 101 unfortunate standees) were clad in the new, rather simpler Go-Ahead seat moquette introduced in the interim and which was being applied to refurbished buses (including MAL 39 back from fire damage). MAL 55 also received a seat retrim to this pattern and a repaint with the now-standard white roof, MAL 35 following in March and MALs 34, 45, 41, 54 and 60 by May to fulfil the requirements of the 436, which as a retained contract required refurbished buses.

Six of Selkent's discarded Citaros returned to Dawson Rentals were taken on lease by Arriva London North for planned increases

Right: **Within the period of artic operation on the 12, a second attempt was made to make it a little easier for buses to sidestep the roiling traffic making its way round Parliament Square by giving them their own right-turn lane into Whitehall. It also made photographers' jobs a bit easier, as nearsides were less likely to get hampered! However, at midday on 12 November 2007 Camberwell's MAL 88 (BX54 UDC) is bagged with no impediment. Snapping the things as they began to turn was an art in and of itself, as the angle of the one half of the bus could blow a clean shot of the second, and vice versa!**
Author

to the 38 (three buses plus one spare) and 149 (one plus one spare) from 19 May. MA 161-166 (skipping three available contiguous numbers, unfortunately) were formerly Selkent 23005, 23006, 23008, 23012, 23015 and 23021, all but the last of them being picked up from Plumstead on 12 April and MA 166 following in May. Until they were ready, MA 125 and 126 were transferred from Edmonton to Ash Grove and MA 73 from Lea Valley to Edmonton, engineering spares making up the numbers.

Finally came the Mayoral election, held on 1 May 2008. Ken Livingstone's bottomless appetite for 'other people's money' had shown no signs of ceasing, his latest wheeze being to soak drivers of 4x4s for £25 when they crossed the Congestion Charge border. Boris Johnson would rather the Western Extension be scrapped altogether, heedless of the loss of revenue that was usually earmarked to go into expanding the bus network. After a runoff, Boris Johnson won and took office from 5 May. His promise to

Right: **Refurbishment has taken the place of the Aldenham overhaul for buses spanning two five-year contract terms (or seven if performance has been above par). The 436's batch of MALs at London Central were the only London artics at all to go through this treatment, and in their case were distinguishable by the new seat moquette they received to match new deliveries to London Central and London General. The livery managed to retain the charcoal skirt, but it would not be much longer before TfL outlawed any livery embellishments at all. The new moquette can be seen on the wheelchair backrest through the window of MAL 43 (BD52 LMV) at Vauxhall on 7 February 2010 while short-working to Hyde Park Corner.**
Author

Left: **Transfers of London buses are an everyday occurrence, but since privatisation a middleman has crept in, which takes its own cut during the process. In the case of the artics the intermediary was invariably Dawson Rentals, and when Stagecoach didn't need a proportion of its artics once the 453 had been lost to London General, they returned to the lessor. However, Arriva could still use a few and took six; they were tacked onto the end of the MA fleetnumber series (albeit skipping two) as MAs 161-166. Not all were used, but MA 162 (LX03 HCE), formerly 23006 and still displaying that number, fits in nicely as a Lea Valley bus as it plies the 73 through Marble Arch on 14 September 2009.**
Malcolm Audsley

eradicate bendy buses coincided with the tenders for the 507 and 521 coming up again after their two extra years had run out. Also coming up, without having had the benefit of a two-year extension, was the 38, although in May the 25 and 73 were both given two more years with their incumbents, which left no more routes coming up before October 2009; unless, that is, their contracts were tinkered with. Coincident with this was the Mayor's invitation to the public and manufacturers from 4 July to design a 21st-century Routemaster which he intended to have in service by May 2012, when his first term would be due to end.

Not service buses as such but rather an outlet for the first artics displaced from TfL requirements, thirteen of the ex-Selkent Citaros that had not reinforced Arriva London North were leased from Dawson Rentals by E&HCT, a collaboration between Ealing and Hackney Community Transports that had won a four-year works contract within the Olympic Park building site commencing on 14 April. They were numbered in an MCA class and painted all-over white, some of the work being done by Evobus at Ash Grove and Clapton as well as at Southall.

Now that West Ham was operational, the 25 was transferred in from Rainham on

Left: **One last inter-company transfer took former Stagecoach 23024 and rechristened it EA 11084 (LX03 HDH) for a new career with First London on the 207. Looking indistinguishable from the rest, helpfully due to the all-red livery it received when with East London matching the one always specified by First, it is seen on 28 November 2011. The location is the new bus station outside the Shepherd's Bush end of Westfield White City, the massive and immediately popular shopping mall opened on 15 October 2008.**
Terry Wong Min

18 May (a Sunday conversion for a change, the night 25s coming over during the small hours) allowing the latter to become a maintenance and storage site again. This allowed 23029 and 23030, two of the four ex-Selkent buses added in February, to come off service, joining twelve returned to Dawson Rentals during May. 23038 did not join them, owing to still being out of action through fire damage incurred on 29 September 2007, and since sent to Caetano for repair work.

The 12 was another artic route to gain a boost, London Central increasing its PVR from 29 to 31 on 17 May. Camberwell too was expecting to pull reinforcements from Dawson Rentals, but took loans from Waterloo, MALs 10 and 25 featuring during June and July. It helped that Go-Ahead MALs all had common blind sets by now; this also allowed Carnival perennial 436X, operated this year as every one since 2004 by Waterloo, could now show blinds rather than slipboards. To this end MAL 20 helped out on the 12 during August while fellow Waterloo MAL 1 was used on the 453 on 11 August.

The first indicator that bendy buses were now persona non grata under the new Mayor was the amendment of the tender specification of routes 507 and 521 as 12-metre single-decks and the 38 as double-decks. Though TfL was mindful of the cost implications of having to increase PVRs substantially, cost comparisons for the retention of artics were also sought from bidders. Even so, the 12 escaped the noose for two more years, on paper at least, with a contract extension implemented in August.

After a prolonged period advertising the University of East London, 23033 and 23034 lost their adverts in August 2008; 23034 merited a full repaint with white roof, but 23033 only had the front repainted red. All of East London's Citaros had had their blue skirts repainted red since the takeover by Macquarie, only 23031 having been the beneficiary of a full repaint and Routemaster-registered 23077 the last to lose its skirt.

Much work had been done over the past few years transforming the patch of waste ground alongside the A3220 (formerly the M41 West Cross Route) into a massive shopping centre known as the Westfield after its Australian conglomerate owner. The old Shepherd's Bush Green layover point at the top end of Caxton Road had closed in April 2004 to be subsumed beneath construction, a new stand being carved out between the two Shepherd's Bush stations. From 29 November, four weeks after the opening of Westfield on 30 October, this was opened up via a perimeter road to reach a new bus station at the White City end of the complex, where terminating buses would stand, and on blinds the whole was collectively known as 'White City' without qualifiers that might have been useful, like 'Westfield Shopping Centre' – bafflingly, TfL prohibited store names from being shown on blinds at all! The 207 was one of the routes thus altered on 29 November and the only artic-operated one to do so; it merited an extra bus on the PVR.

Arriva London North's 'new' MAs were ready by the autumn; MA 166 entered service at Lea Valley on 29 September and MA 164

followed by 17 December. On 1 October one of the two ex-Selkent artics secured by London Central for the 12's PVR increase entered service; 23030 was now MAL 120, in all-over red. Further Go-Ahead examples refurbished by the autumn were MALs 37, 38, 40, 42, 44, 49, 50, 51, 56, 59 and 61. The final cross-company transfer to affect the artic fleet was that of former Selkent 23024, leased to First from Dawson Rentals in November under the number EA 11084. Allocated to Hayes for the 207's boost by one, it was also known to operate from Willesden Junction on the 18 and was photographed doing so.

The 'New Bus for London' competition closed on 19 September for a couple of months' worth of judging between more than 700 entries. To the predictable criticism, this took precedence over a raft of intended transport programmes, which were cancelled by the Mayor during the autumn, including, on 27 November, the western extension to the Congestion Charge. London Travelwatch was already making representations over the intended withdrawal of the 507's and 521's MALs, citing their passenger-carrying capacity (without mentioning that so few of those were seated) and the cost of replacing them. As an advance measure of sorts, the penalty fare was increased on 11 January 2009 from £20 to £50.

November saw the first contract awards for the post-bendy era. The 507 and 521 were retained by London General but with 47 12m single-deckers replacing the 28 artics (the 507's PVR increasing from 9 to 15 and that on the 521 from 19 to 32). The colossal increase and the introduction of a weekend service on the 507 was tempered by the fact that the open-boarding aspect was to be retained on each route, thus missing the point of one of the key antagonisms against the artics. A similar massive boost affected the 38, which was retained by Arriva London North but with its 47 artics replaced by 72 double-deckers. The Red Arrows' contract date was 30 May 2009 and that of the 38 fell on 18 July, with both dates liable to slip contingent upon vehicle delivery. On 19 December the Mayor announced the winners of the '21st-century Routemaster' competition – Capoco Design and a consortium of Aston Martin and Foster & Partners; their designs would be melded and offered to manufacturers who would tender to build it. The reactions of London Travelwatch and of Labour's transport spokesperson Val Shawcross were predictably sceptical, the latter pooh-poohing the whole exercise as a study in vanity, but it proved that each Mayor was able to display a remarkably equal level of bloody-mindedness as regards the practical fulfilment of his ambitions!

First's EAs were treated to iBus by mid-December; MAL 43 and 58 were two more London Central artics at New Cross refurbished and repainted in November and MALs 36 and 43 followed suit in December. Go-Ahead held on to its charcoal-skirted livery jealously and was the last TfL contractor to give up a non-red livery; Waterloo's were left alone as their contracts were not long for this world. Although the 'Borismaster', as it was inevitably nicknamed, was intended to go into production in 2012, the schedule of bendy bus contract expiry meant that it would not necessarily be a direct replacement for them.

CHAPTER TEN

2009

The year began with the local treatment of East London's artics to iBus equipment; one of them was 23038, repaired finally by February and returned to service.

On 5 February Arriva London North ordered 57 new Wrightbus Gemini 2 DL integral double-deckers to add to five already coming for evaluation, plus eighteen Enviro400s that together would form a mixed allocation on the 38. The 38's MAs were henceforth on borrowed time, MA 98 not doing the type's PR any favours when it got stuck during heavy snowfall on 2 February. The weather was adverse enough that Arriva London North took its buses off the road for the rest of the day, not chancing to put any artics out at all and substituting a handful of double-deckers on the 29 and 149 instead. Closure of the Tottenham Court

Road left turn for Crossrail construction from 3 January had already obliged the 38 to divert southbound down the length of Shaftesbury Avenue to and from Cambridge Circus.

The refurbishment and repaint programme of London Central MAs drew to a close in 2009, with MALs 32 and 52 done in January, MALs 48 and 53 in February, MALs 33, 47 and 57 in March and MAL 46, the last, completed in May. The London Central logos with Cutty Sark motif were left alone on their glass panels rather than being replaced by Go-Ahead's newer logo. Bendies were often likened to accordions due to their bellows-like canvas attachments dividing the two sections, but a short-lived advert applied to Arriva's MA 146 for a local competition placed accordion-key graphics on the edge of the bellows, which remained when the rest of the advert was stripped off.

Right: **The Routemaster registrations will probably go on forever, even though the buses they once adorned have been consigned mostly to fate. After four years on the Arriva MAs, they were redistributed again between newer classes; thus MA 17 regained its BX04 MXR mark and sent 217 CLT to an Enviro400. The home-made nature of the plate is evident on this 13 February 2011 view at Wood Green, showing some spacing that would antagonise the good authorities of Swansea.** *Author*

East London had perhaps got rid of too many of its bendies, given the extreme pressure on the 25, and took back two from Dawson Rentals in February; these were 23019 and 23029.

Forty-nine Citaros were ordered by Go-Ahead in February for the replacement of the 507's and 521's MALs – despite being on the same chassis, these were rigid 12-metre versions. Already the future of the Red Arrow examples was being thought about, MAL 5 paying a visit to Go-Ahead North East at Gateshead between 8 and 15 February; while there, it was known as 9166. The entire batch of 31 was advertised for sale in March through Lombard, part of RBS. To ward off already shrill voices being raised by the likes of London Travelwatch and Val Shawcross against replacing the bendy buses, TfL published the cost figures for their removal from the first three routes, which with the increase factored in, stood at £21.1m per year against new artics at £19.9m and retaining the existing buses at £17.8m. If contract terms were adhered to, the last artics to come off would be those on the 436 and 453, both in February 2013, but the next, the 149, wasn't due for another twenty months. A timetable was nonetheless set when in May the Mayor instructed that all bendy buses be removed by the end of 2011, which would necessitate tinkering with the contracts. This was poetic justice in a way, as this was exactly what had happened to the last Routemaster routes' contracts to speed up the process of fulfilling an arbitrary date of the end of 2005. Accordingly, in June the 38's contract was extended beyond 18 July to match the delivery and entry into service of its new double-deckers, which by that point was envisaged as 14 November.

One of the 149's additions, MA 163, was put into service in March, leaving three left to do in a rather protracted process; MA 162 followed suit in April. MAs 161 and 165, however, were sent back to Dawson Rentals without seeing any use. The second-hand ones plus MA 1-44 were earmarked for withdrawal upon the conversion of the 38 to DW and T operation, and to underscore their fading fortunes, the first five with Routemaster marks lost them to year-old Enviro400s during May. MA 80's 480 CLT went onto a car in June. The last remnants of the old Stagecoach livery on artics departed in June when 23077 finally had its blue skirt painted over red; the livery as a whole was declining rapidly.

Below: **In its element on Waterloo Bridge is MAL 17 (BX02 YZA). The date is 10 July 2009, and this summer would see the two Red Arrow routes herald the replacement of the first artics.** *Jimmy Sheng*

On 5 June TfL announced that six manufacturers were invited to bid for the contract to build what was now referred to as the 'New Bus for London'. These were Alexander Dennis, Hispano, Mercedes-Benz, Optare, Scania and Wrightbus, though Scania and Mercedes-Benz withdrew as early as August, worried about the timescale. Hispano and Optare followed suit by year's end, leaving two British manufacturers to duke it out. It would hardly have been good for PR had Londoners' new bus, which was supposed to embody the best of British culture and provide work for British labour, been designed and manufactured by foreign concerns! Even so, the design was heavily watered down by this stage to resemble a Routemaster only in the inclusion of a rear platform. The Unite union took the

opportunity to protest the removal of bendies, not for any inconvenience to passengers of course but on pay grounds due to the extra that had been allotted to artic drivers since their introduction.

On 30 May the new five-year terms for the 507 and 521 took effect with the existing buses, as did that of the 38 on 18 July. But the first artic route to receive its new buses was the 507, which on the 25th was converted to MECs, the code for the fifty new fixed Citaros ordered for London General and delivered just about in time. Much was made of the photocall held by the Mayor the previous afternoon at Mandela Way, during which he reiterated his intention to dispose of all the bendies by the end of 2011 and send them 'back to their spiritual home, an airfield in the Midlands'.

Above: **The section of Lower Clapton Road along which MA 79 (BX05 UWY) is seen passing on 18 July 2009 is unkindly dubbed Murder Mile, though daytime seems safe enough for photographers of buses, who often feel themselves treated like ne'er-do-wells! Time was almost up for the 38's bendies after the statutory five years, and probably for the better, all told.**
Jimmy Sheng

Waterloo thus opened on Saturdays and Sundays to accommodate the 507's new weekend service, a plan to outstation part of its allocation at Mandela Way having to be postponed until the 521 was done on 29 August. Although New Cross loaned MALs 52 and 59 to Waterloo for the 521 from 20 July just in case all the MECs didn't make it on time – and they very nearly didn't – Waterloo released enough artics to top up long-standing shortages at New Cross (MALs 10 and 25) and Camberwell (MALs 1, 5, 12, 20, 28 and 30); the 453 also needed help. Loans from Waterloo to Camberwell had been common in the earlier part of the year, MALs 4, 15, 21 and 28 having been sighted on the 12 during the spring. Summer specials saw the final appearance of artics on the 406F for Derby Day (MALs 1, 6, 8, 30 and 31 doing the honours) while strike action on 9/10 July saw EA help on the 18 and East London examples for O2-Charlton extras.

On 29 August (though to take account of the Bank Holiday, with effect from 1 September) the 521 followed suit. Waterloo reverted to Monday-to-Friday operation with the move of the 507's weekend allocation to Mandela Way, whch took six of the 31 buses allocated to the 521. None of the MECs carried Red Arrow fleetnames, the name

Left: **On 31 August 2009 Willesden Junction's EA 11001 (LK53 FAA) crawls along the Harrow Road, stuffed to the windscreens with revellers bound for this year's incarnation of the Notting Hill Carnival; but take a look at what's tucked in behind it; Volvo VNL 32215 (LT52 WTY) on a guest working seconded from Alperton. Double-deckers would shadow artics on Carnival day throughout their tenure on the 18.**
Terry Wong Min

Right: **Lea Valley's MA 47 (BX04 MYR) lies wrecked on 15 September 2009 after a head-on collision with VLW 120 in Tottenham High Road that injured six. Both vehicles were repaired.** *Author's collection*

Below: **Lea Valley's MA 2 (BX04 MWY) heads up the Essex Road on 18 July 2009 en route to Seven Sisters. Points off for not displaying a running number. The bus, though not its passengers, can be grateful that from September the 73's contract was extended for two more years, although from Saturday 14 November passengers would have a double-deck alternative again up this thoroughfare when the 38 was converted.** *Jimmy Sheng*

effectively being dropped although MAL 30, one of the top-ups, continued to carry it. The MECs also took over the seasonal Notting Hill Carnival 436X express, though existing New Cross MALs were added to the 436's allocation on both afternoons to get revellers there and back. During October the Red Arrow batch was sent for storage, barring MALs 1 and 12, which remained in service, MAL 1 at Mandela Way until late November when it joined MAL 12 at Camberwell. MAL 7 was evaluated by Wilts & Dorset during early September and MAL 120 paid a visit to

Brighton & Hove on 14/15 October, returning between 10 November and 14 January 2010 as the company expressed interest in taking some for routes serving the University.

The 38's intended DWs began type training on 1 September. On the 5th the 73's contract was extended for two more years, and on the 15th Lea Valley's MA 47 was severely damaged when it collided with VLW 120 in Tottenham High Road while working on the 149 at about seven o'clock in the morning; it was pushed into a building. It was towed to Truck Align for repair. East London's 23077

Right: **Of all twelve artic routes, the 38 was surely least suited to them and their imposition the most resented, so it was doubly good for morale that not only should it revert to double-deck at the earliest opportunity but also that an absolutely gargantuan PVR increase was implemented, bringing it to seventy vehicles scheduled. This was muttered at for being profligate in the extreme, but the gamble was worth taking, as the shortfall was easily redeployed once the 38's needs had been rationalised to just about what they had been when RMLs operated it. On 14 November 2009, the first day of the new contract, DW 217 (LJ09 STX), like its fellows based at a reactivated Clapton, waits for the off at Victoria.** *Author*

hit a skip on 16 November while running dead to West Ham and was also badly damaged. While working on the N29 on 22 July, Edmonton's MA 135 hit both a shelter and a tree at Wood Green.

The conversion of the 38 to DW and T operation on 14 November was a more visible indication than any so far that bendies were on their way out. Clapton was restored to full use, the 242 and 393 coming back with it, and MA 77-123 were placed in store at Ash Grove. After being fitted with blind sets covering the 29, 73 and 148 (albeit with single-line destinations only) they were reallocated to Lea Valley, where they replaced MA 1-44 on the 73 and 149 over two weeks. MA 124-126 settled at Edmonton, allowing MAs 73 and 76 to return to Lea Valley and after this was all done MA 162-164 and 166 were then MOT'd and went off lease. November was a good month for Arriva London North, as the contract announcement for the 149 let

them keep it, specifying a PVR of 35 new double-deckers to replace its 27 MALs. And still with this company, the 29 and N29 were extended for two years, though conversion from artic would follow before that. One of its motors, MA 135, was evaluated by Isle of Man Transport (Bus Vannin) between 7-21 December, and three more, MAs 9, 12 and 40 were tried out in Liverpool from 19 December in advance of a total of twenty being earmarked for Arriva North West. One of the 38's new buses, DW 261, took the RM registration from MA 61 in December.

Below: **The 38's MAs were sent en bloc to Lea Valley to take over the 73 and 149 from their 04-reg. counterparts, exemplifying age-related cascading even within this otherwise route-bound class. Shoreditch has transformed itself from a down-at-heel district on the City fringes to a vibrant quarter set off by the new Overground rail service, and just south of its bridge on 7 August 2010 is MA 84 (BU05 VFG).** *Author*

CHAPTER ELEVEN

2010

Crossrail works at Tottenham Court Road Station obliged the temporary curtailment of the 25 there from 16 January, other routes having to pick up the slack into Oxford Circus; the 73 was also contorted eastbound away from the eastern half of Oxford Street beyond Oxford Circus.

January saw the 18's contract awarded back to First London with the promise of 48 double-deckers replacing its 32 artics on 13 November; 53 buses were ordered and confirmed a little later as Volvo B9TLs (VNs). For the 149, Arriva placed an order for forty more Wrightbus Gemini 2 integrals to arrive in July. The four remaining ex-East London MAs were collected by Dawson Rentals in February, having been spruced up ready for them. MA 40 was loaned from Arriva Merseyside to Arriva Midlands in March to try out in Leicester.

From 10 April the 207's contract was extended with its incumbent operator for two more years, which did not affect the timetable set out for the removal of all artics. The figure of £24.9m had been bandied about as the cost of their replacement, added to which was £11m for development and construction of the New Bus for London prototypes, which, it was announced on 23 December, would be built by Wrightbus. Amid all this spending on so-called vanity projects rather than other cancelled schemes, small bites were taken out of operations in compensation, PVRs going down by a bus here, a bus there; for instance, in an ongoing effort to reduce the perceived number of buses in Oxford Street going about allegedly empty, several routes were curtailed short of this extremely busy thoroughfare. The 25 was altered so that only every other bus proceeded further west than Holborn Circus; Crossrail construction work bedevilling the Tottenham Court Road area was a good enough justification for this. Its PVR was cut from 44 to 39, although keeping it where it was might have done something about persistent overcrowding. Additionally, on 27 March another attempt was made to smooth traffic flow across Piccadilly Circus by introducing a westbound contraflow, used by the 38 amongst others. Crossrail also obliged the 436's stand at Paddington to be altered from 3 July.

In May the 25's tender award was announced; not only would it be converted to double-deck with a 59-strong PVR, but First would be returning from 25 June 2011. Surprisingly, 23072 and 23077 were repainted during May and 23062 by September.

Arriva London North MA 135 performed a route trial in Cardiff during March; two more (9 and 12) joined MA 40 on trials in Leicester during May, while four more lost

Below: **The imperative to all-red livery reached its nadir in the first decade of the 21st century, even skirts now being declared outlaw. East London's artics gradually complied, and an example now in all-red is 23059 (LX04 LBP), which on 9 October 2010 is espied coming up to Tottenham Court Road where it has been turned.** *Author*

Left: **On 16 April 2010 MA 92 (BX55 FUJ) works southward through Stoke Newington; ignore the CT code because it's operating out of Lea Valley. The 149 was converted back to double-deck on 16 October and MA 92 ended its days in Malta.** *Terry Wong Min*

their RM registrations during May, three Ts and one DW being the beneficiaries. That left just MA 70, which surrendered 70 CLT in July. Living up to the stereotype, MA 54 caught fire on its way into Lea Valley garage on 17 June at midday; the fire-suppression system activated but could not prevent the fire spreading and the Fire Brigade were the ones that put it out. It was towed to Evobus at Southall for repair, in the same month as MA 10 and 25 were sold to Arriva Midlands.

As culturally damaging to Malta's identity as bendies had been to that of London was the decision to replace the island's bus network with a corporatised and homogenised version, which Arriva was selected to operate on 31 July; murmurings flew that part of this would be accomplished in a year or so with former London bendies. To this end, MA 100-157 were earmarked for export to Malta, these newer versions being replaced on the 73 and 29 (while they were still artic-operated) by the already decommissioned older ones and those leaving the 149. This route's intended new DWs began delivery from 28 June, boosted by the moving forward of the conversion date to 16 October due to the need to reallocate the route to Tottenham so that Lea Valley could simultaneously take over the 341 from First. Eight more MAs (6, 13, 21, 23, 24, 32, 33 and 41) were chosen to provide transport for the Ryder Cup golf tournament being held in Newport between 1-4 October; they were prepared for the event (including repaint into turquoise Arriva livery) by a Manchester-based Evobus dealer, ENZA Motors, with additional work carried out by Bus & Coach World of Blackburn, which included modifying the gearbox so that first gear was retained on the incline

Left: **The strategy by Arriva to fill their newest acquisition on Malta with ex-London artics at least offered some semblance of a future to buses that were otherwise nowhere near time-expired even by modern standards. Accordingly, during 2011 MAs 100-157 were taken off service and replaced on the 29, 73 and 149 by lower-numbered examples. On 20 July 2010 Wood Green's MA 141 (BX55 FXE) heads north through Turnpike Lane; it would ship out to Malta the following June.** *Author*

to the VIP coach park; following this they would be converted to dual-door and moved on to Arriva North West to replace former SLWs off the Runcorn guided busway. Arriva itself was sold to Deutsche Bahn, the sale being finalised on 31 August.

Artic number five to suffer total destruction by fire was Lea Valley's MA 122, which at 8.30 in the morning of 4 September, to mark the sixth anniversary of the conversion to artic of the 73, was captured on film burning to a crisp in that route's stand and stop at Victoria bus station. The fire started in the engine compartment and devoured the interior in

no time. MA 158 was thus added to the Malta contingent, the first examples of which had already started to go away for repaint and retrim at Hants & Dorset during August. Recertification work for MAs to be restored to service in their place was subdivided between a large variety of concerns, numbering Evobus in Coventry, ENZA Motors, Rossetts Commercials (at three locations: Eastbourne, Worthing and Aldershot) and Arriva's own facility at Cleckheaton. Once they came back to town they had their iBus and ticket machines swapped from 05- and 55-reg MAs marked for Malta.

The schedule for bendy replacement rolled on. In September the 12 was awarded, remaining with London Central but with 41 new double-deckers to replace its 31 artics from 5 November 2011. Go-Ahead was already considering the future for some of its artics, sending MAL 112 to Plymouth Citybus between 24-28 August. Some of Arriva's new DWs entered service early, taking over the 76 during September so that drivers for the 149 could be trained on them.

There were just two more artic tenders to be awarded, those of the 436 and 453, but since they were not due till February 2013 and politics dictated the vehicles be replaced by the end of 2011, their tenders were brought forward and combined into one new tranche (371A). Meanwhile, although the fixed Citaros on the RV1 had served without overmuch difficulty, their time was now up too and they were removed on 7 October.

Stagecoach made a triumphant return to the capital on 14 October, buying back East London Bus Group for £59.8m; ELBG had won little since the takeover by Macquarie and had been beset by strike action. While the livery remained the all-over red settled upon by ELBG, Stagecoach fleetnames quickly made their return.

The 16th saw the 149 assume double-deck operation again, transferring from Lea Valley to Tottenham with new DW 298-336. As with the former Routemaster routes, the opportunity to restore them to their former extent now that the reason for their conversion had been overturned was wasted,

the 149's northern terminus remaining at Edmonton Green. Far from being withdrawn, or from the obvious option of providing a link beyond Stoke Newington to Hackney, the accompanying 349 was now withdrawn south of Stoke Newington, making it even more pointless than it was to begin with! Additionally, the new double-deck runout was slightly too large for Tottenham, eight buses having to overnight it at Lea Valley until 5 February 2011. The displaced MAs were stored at Ash Grove, seven being used

Right: **For all the rigidity of allocations when a dedicated fleet is supplied to one route only, the artics actually did some shifting over their careers, and certainly in their latter days. The withdrawal of the newest Arriva MAs to supply Malta obliged the 29 to restock itself with the buses taken off the 149 at the same time, and accordingly on 7 November 2010 MA 26 (BX04 MYB) is now an Edmonton bus, seen at Goodge Street.** *Author*

to provide a free shuttle to and from the ExCel Centre for the World Travel Market between 8-11 November; eighteen more, including six Edmonton examples from the 29, were stripped of ticket machines and iBus equipment in order to be refurbished to Euro 5 standard for Malta. Older MAs 4, 8, 29, 31, 35, 37 and 38 replaced them, followed in November by MAs 15-17 and 22 replacing MAs 131 and 134-136. MAs 2, 26 and 28 were allocated to Edmonton in December as MAs 125-130 left.

On 13 November the 18 lost its artics for new Wright-bodied Volvo B9TLs VN 37890-37942; the N18 also assumed the new buses on transfer from Alperton. Some of them were broken in on the 18 as tube strike extras ten days previously. All of the 53-registered batch of EAs plus four of the ex-East London examples were withdrawn, second-hand EAs 11000 and 11084 surviving to join the 207's fleet at Hayes. Some of the displaced ones were stored at a Dawson Rentals yard at Bedford with the Citaro artics used by

Below: **Seen under preparation for Malta is the former MA 138 (BX55 FWZ) at London Truck & Bus during 2010; this was one of the first to be repainted into Arriva corporate aquamarine (as with the London buses, no stone scoop was ever carried). With Arriva Malta it became BUS 217.** *Dave Brundrit*

Left: **Willesden Junction remained the base for the 18 following its conversion back to double-deck operation on 13 November 2010, though the artic-length pits were now somewhat superfluous. On 13 February 2011 Wright-bodied Volvo B9TL VN 37936 (BF60 UVH) picks up its first passengers of this round trip at Euston. The subsequent withdrawal of First from London has altered this bus's identity; it is now Metroline VW 1888.** *Author*

Menzies on airside work and those that had assisted Olympic Park construction for Hackney & Ealing Community Transport but which had also now come off service. It wasn't just London!

The Western Extension of the Congestion Charge was discontinued after 24 December (the Mayor having promised to do so as quickly as 8 May), but the the cost of entering the existing area increased to £10 with effect from 4 January 2011. However, five of the twelve bendy routes had now lost their artics, with the other seven still slated to lose them during 2011. One such tender, awarded in December, was that of the 73,

on which fifty-one new double-deckers (including twenty hybrids) were scheduled to replace the existing forty-three artics from 3 September 2011, while one of Go-Ahead's November order for the 12 comprised forty-two Enviro400s and First placed an order in December for sixty-five Wright-bodied Volvo B9TLs (VNs) for the 25. If people wanted to see bendy-buses in strength after the end of the forthcoming year, they would have to go to Malta, where Arriva's takeover was rubber-stamped on 20 November for a 3 July 2011 start. With an eye on future disposals, Go-Ahead sent MAL 98 on loan to Go North East over Christmas.

Left: **Blinds were just one of the aspects of London buses that changed in the 2000s and not for the better; no matter how much power blinds relieved drivers of a particularly onerous task of winding through destinations, sometimes they didn't work; if MA 89 (BX55 FWA) is actually in service when captured at Hyde Park Corner on 20 August 2011, it's going the wrong way!** *Author*

CHAPTER TWELVE

2011

Below: **When Whitehall is out of commission for whatever reason, buses are re-routed via Waterloo instead, and such has befallen the 453 service on 13 February 2011, probably for a demonstration, an irritatingly frequent practice which bedevils orderly movement in central London on, it seems, most Saturdays nowadays. The bus is Mandela Way's MAL 104 (BD57 WDP).** *Author*

The last year of artics in London bowed with Arriva's order for 37 Wrightbus Gemini 2DLs and 20 Volvo B5LHs to replace them from the 73 on 3 September. Although most artic routes stayed where they'd been transferred, this one would need to ship out, Stamford Hill being chosen as the recipient, only a short run away from where the 73 was now going to terminate, once again at Stoke Newington as before. The total for Malta was revised to 57 (MAs 100-121, 123-157), of which MA 123, in full aquamarine Arriva livery with cream front, was already on the island being used as a trainer. The last of the Malta-bound Citaros, MAs 124, 153 and 155-157, came out of service in March, the replacement early examples spanning MAs 2-4, 7, 8, 11, 15-18, 20, 22, 26-31, 34-39 and 42-44. MAs 54 and 122, or what was left of their burnt-out carcasses, were used for spare parts.

First restored EAs 11005 and 11009 to service in January, though the process of returning Citaros to Dawson Rentals had begun in earnest and examples drifted away in dribs and drabs for the next six months. On 15 February MA 91, working the N29 down Camden Road, collided with Metroline's Enviro400 TE 926 crossing the York Way junction; the Citaro came off worse but both vehicles were ultimately repaired.

And then there were two. Tranche 371A, that of the 436 and 453 combined, was awarded in February with London Central taking both. The 436's 26 artics would be replaced by 32 new double-deckers, with the 453's 23 artics giving way to 35 new double-deckers. Of the 67 new buses, 31 would be hybrids. All that remained now was to set dates to convert the 29 and 207 within their existing contract terms and order the vehicles for them, and that would be that.

Arriva officially disposed of the Malta expats-to-be in March, though they would go away in batches between February and May after being prepared, the final part of the process being fitment of Euro 5 engines in Oxford. During March Go-Ahead sent MAL 95 to Go-Ahead North-East on loan, Mandela Way taking MA 70 from Camberwell in exchange to add an original-fronted version to the newer examples for variety. In April Go-Ahead placed orders for double-decks which would include those for the 436 and 453; of the 31 hybrids, sixteen were Volvo B5LHs and fifteen Alexander Dennis E40Hs, the new chassis code for a significant revision of the Enviro400H chassis to comply with European Whole Type legislation). Diesel orders would bring the E class of the corresponding E40D up to 245 members and the WVL class to 454; which garage would receive which chassis would be firmed up closer to the November date of each contract.

By the summer the dates were firmed up for the last two artic routes; the 29 would go on 26 November and it can be no coincidence that 10 December was chosen for the 207's conversion, meaning that the previous day would mark exactly six years since their nemesis, the Routemaster, plied the streets for the last time on normal service. It was at this point that First ordered the 207's new fleet, with a few eyes opened this time in that it was 39 Scania OmniCitys, the all-Polish option that had proven popular with East London Bus Group and the French owners of London United and Sovereign before, just as quickly, interest died down and London operators began buying British again. The reason in this case was that only Scania felt it could meet the delivery deadline.

One last Citaro artic blotted the class's copybook on 29 June by going up in flames while working on the 73 at Stamford Hill Broadway and writing itself off only two months before it would have been withdrawn anyway; this was MA 82, and that made six fire casualties. All were engine fires, not a phenomenon isolated to British operators. Not to let the unfortunate MA off the hook, but a DW from the batch immediately prior

Above: One of the most widely-publicised criticisms of the bendy buses was that they were a menace to cyclists. Undoubtedly true, but no more so than just about any other form of motor transport in the pitiless and aggressive hurly-burly that characterises traffic in the capital. Still, the cyclist waiting for MA 65 (BX04 NCU) to haul its full length round the sharp turn from Gower Street into New Oxford Street on 26 March 2011 would be well served to step back a little, lest the vehicle squash him and his steed alike. *Author*

to that about to undergo delivery for the 73 suffered an electrical fire on the same day.

At Go-Ahead, MAL 95 came back to Mandela Way in April, allowing MAL 70 to return to Camberwell, but second-hand MAL 120 was disposed of. On 12 July Lombard Finance held an auction to attempt to dispose of the 22 ex-Red Arrow MALs it had been keeping at Bruntingthorpe airfield since their withdrawal; only six had gone on to further service, two remained doggedly in action on the 12 out of Camberwell and one was beyond help. On 3 May the 38 and 73 swapped stands at Victoria bus station.

The 25's conversion was straightforward enough, seven years minus one day after it had gone over. First's new buses, operating from Lea Interchange (LI) were VNs 36101-36165 – 59 scheduled and six spares – and were occasionally joined by the DN-class Enviro400s bought at the same time for the 26 and 30, two more routes taken from Stagecoach in a one-two-three punch that staggered the recently returned operator. The 25 was Stagecoach's last artic route, it now bowing out of our story with the onward dispatch of the artics to Dawson Rentals from whence they came.

Left: **The last summer of artics on the 453, and on 20 August 2011 MAL 104 (BD57 WDP) does its thing for the tourists in Parliament Square who are probably wondering why there's not a single Routemaster present in the locations that countless forms of media have told them to expect there. After withdrawal MAL 104 went to Brighton & Hove as their no 111.** *Author*

Right: **It's a shame no moves were made to reunite sections of routes created upon conversion to bendy-bus operation. The 453, upon the removal of its artics on 24 September 2011, thus retained its rather wasteful overlap along the Old Kent Road and continued to prevent the 53 from taking its passengers further towards their central London workplaces than Whitehall. The balance of the 453's new E-class Enviro400s were not ready, so PVLs stepped in for some weeks. On the first day we see one of each at the Deptford bridge stand; E 165 (SN11 BGO) and PVL 304 (PJ02 RFZ), both out of Mandela Way. The dumbing-down of blinds and liveries is all too evident by the time of the Enviro's generation.** *Author*

One last set of transfers during August bought MAs 48, 49, 65, 66 and 71 a little more time through their transfer from Lea Valley to Edmonton, which gave up MAs 3, 8, 28, 30 and 36 in exchange. Seven years to the day after the infamous Black Friday came the reversion of the 73 to double-deck on 3 September. While the new allocation of 51 buses, working out of Stamford Hill from this day, was intended to be worked by DWs 428-464 and HVs 27-46, not all of the DWs had been delivered or fitted out completely, despite Wright setting up an additional production line, so existing VLWs of both lengths available had to deputise for a few weeks; these at least showed some effort in the blind boxes. Although MAs 80-87 were kept behind for a while to service this year's incarnation of the World Travel Market at ExCel and MAs 45, 59, 63, 64, 75 and 78 passed to Edmonton to bolster the 29 while it lasted, thirty more were withdrawn and, once relieved of their radios, ticket machines and Oyster gear at Lea Valley, were divided between two storage sites belonging to Arriva Midlands: Coalville and Derby. MA 93 became a Malta bus, being refurbished by Rossett prior to making the sea voyage.

The conversion of the 453 found itself moved up from 19 November (the contract date) to 24 September, even though not all of its allocation of E40Ds (E 163-201) had made it in time to be in place. Although the 453 was awarded on paper to London Central, with plans laid to transfer the route to New Cross, Mandela Way (a London General garage

within Go-Ahead London) remained open and put into service as many Es as it could muster, with the help of sixteen refurbished PVLs seconded from Camberwell. MALs 110 and 111 were used briefly at Camberwell on the 12 before joining MALs 95-97 at KonectBus in Norfolk. At least the newer Citaros found new work easier than had their forebears, as MALs 98-107 were taken by Brighton & Hove and MALs 108, 109 and 112-119 by Go-Ahead North East.

November 2011 was a banner month for haters of the bendy-bus, three routes discarding the vehicles on near-consecutive weekends of the month. First up (or down) was the 12 on the fifth, seven years to the day after its Routemasters departed. It was to this route that the Volvo versions of the hybrid order bought with this year's allocation of Green Bus funding were to go, numbering WHV 1-16, alongside diesel B9TLs WVL 435-454 to furnish a PVR of 41. These latter did arrive in time, Camberwell running some of them in on the 45. The final two in-service transfers of London bendy-buses saw two of the 12's Citaros transferred to First to shore up the 207 for its last two months; these were MALs 78 and 85 from approximately 18 November and it wasn't felt worth bothering to renumber them or even stick fleetnames on. The rest of the MAL 62-94 batch plus MALs 1 and 12 were collected at Belvedere, from where MALs 62-65 were sold to Brighton & Hove, MAL 92 to KonectBus, MALs 67, 68 and 70-75 to Go-Ahead North East and MAL 94 to Go South Coast on the Isle of Wight.

Above: **Two 'Red Arrow' MALs
survived the purge of their
type from the 507 and 521 and
fought all the way to the end
of artic operation within Go-
Ahead, helping out on routes
12 and 436 where needed.
On 19 March 2011, on the
approaches to the Elephant
& Castle, MAL 12 (BX02 YYT),
stripped of its Red Arrow
logos, is working the 12 out of
Camberwell.** *Graham Smith*

Left: **Hybrids formed at least
part of most double-deck
orders by the time the bendies
were passing out of existence.
The 12's new complement from
5 November 2011 included
sixteen WHVs to accompany
nineteen WVLs, and on
8 March 2012 at Parliament
Square we see Camberwell's
WHV 16 (LJ61 GXP). The short
wheelbase and long rear
overhang of the Wright-bodied
B5LH chassis combine to
produce an almost comically
dumpy appearance; even
though passenger comfort was
substantially improved upon
the conversion back to double-
deck, aesthetics came a distant
second!** *Author*

Left and below left: **The final examples of inter-company artic transfers didn't even bother with new fleetnumbers, First doing quite well with the existing MAL 78 and 85 rather than troubling adding two more members to the EA class (or even including them in the fleetwide SEMA system) for the temporary nature of their stay. Unfortunately, nor was it deemed cost-effective to install blinds, so slipboards have to make do inside the windscreen of MAL 78 (BX54 UDH), seen at Ealing Common on 28 November, and in MAL 85 (BX54 UDP), seen laying over at Hayes By-Pass on 9 December, the class's last day in service.**
Terry Wong Min (left); *Jack Marian* (below left)

On the 19th fell the 436, which continued at New Cross but with an intentional mix of diesels and hybrids to replace its MALs. These were E 208-228 and EH 6-20. That was the end of London Central's participation, and that of Go-Ahead as a whole. Really, with both 36 and 436 now operating the same format of OPO double-deckers, there was no further point in continuing with the 436 at all, but it remained and indeed now enjoyed a PVR on a par with the 36 from which it derived.

Finally for November, on the 26th double-deckers were restored to the 29, which under bendies had gained an unsavoury reputation that it simply hadn't merited before this form of transport was imposed upon it; this author took it twice a day for years over its entire length, and at much the time of day when more than a few of its passengers are likely to be lairy and/or spoiling for a fight, yet never encountered the least bit of trouble. Combined with changes in associated Arriva London South and tendering losses to come in the new year, the reallocation of the 29 back to Wood Green upon its double-decking put Edmonton garage on borrowed time. Towards the end, the bendies looked unkempt, with a fifth unable to display full blinds other than a number. Bolstered during November by the return of the World Travel Market MAs, Edmonton's closing roster, exemplifying Arriva London North's last artic commitment, was composed of MAs 7, 11, 15, 16, 18, 22, 26, 27, 29, 21, 34, 37-39, 43-45, 48, 49, 59, 63-66, 71, 75, 78, 80, 81, 83-87, 91, 92 and 94-99; MA 75 was the last one into the garage. Stored again at Coalville or Derby, many of these sales were subsequently added to the Malta fleet.

The 29's new fleet, broken in on existing Wood Green services as they arrived, comprised 47 DWs (465-511) to service a 42-strong PVR. They took assistance where needed from Wood Green's existing fleet of VLWs, which still carried the blinds they had when they were obliged to leave the route nearly six years earlier. As the 29's contract was not to expire until as far off as April 2013, this mid-contract type change underscored the Mayor's desire to get shot of the bendies before the end of 2011, and that had to all intents and purposes been accomplished. Politically-motivated? Of course it was, but the one good turn of the previous occupant of City Hall deserved another, and for all the massive cost to the taxpayer, it was probably for the good; surely it wasn't as if the money wouldn't have been spent, wasted or not, on something equally as contentious. £7.4m a year was now being saved on fare evasion.

Left: **19 November 2011** saw another bendy route replenished wholesale with new double-deckers without any alteration to its format; the 436 would have done just as well simply being folded back into its parent 36 as a much-increased New Cross allocation with a welcome extension back to Lewisham. During mid-morning, hybrid EH 13 (SN61 DBU) swings into Vauxhall bus station. *Author*

Left: **Another of the older MAs that finished out their days on the 29 in 2011 is MA 35 (BX04 NDV)**, seen at Wood Green on 3 July unfortunately sporting a N29 blind, even though it's four hours till that night route comes on. The girl boarding doesn't seem unduly traumatised, and for all the criticism of the dumbed-down blinds imposed on passengers in the first decade of the twenty-first century, it's an unhappy truth that the public remain so obstinately brainless that you could have no blinds at all and they'd still bother the poor driver with the same predictable set of questions. *Author*

Left: **Another route earmarked for 100% hybrid operation in the medium term, the 29** replaced its bendies on 26 November 2011 with DWs which could be cascaded within Arriva London North later to replace DLAs and the first of the VLWs. As night falls on 28 January 2012, DW 476 (LJ61 CBY) sets off south from Wood Green Station, where there's plenty of space in the artic-sized bus stop box for it and a couple more buses at least. *Author*

And that brought us to the 207, London's last artic-operated bus route. All that was left in service, ploughing up and down their Uxbridge Road furrow between Shepherd's Bush and Hayes By-Pass, were EAs 11040-11065 (the 207's original batch minus EA 11039) plus former demonstrator EA 11000, ex-Stagecoach transfer EA 11084 and the two London Central refugees which retained their MAL 78 and 85 identities to the finish. SN 36031-36069, the 39 new Scania OmniCitys purchased for the route, arrived in good time from Poland, gathering at Scania's Worksop premises after coming off the boat towards the end of September; all were ready by the end of October and training commenced.

Their introduction would boost the 207's PVR from 26 to 35.

Curiously, the conversion process from artic to conventional buses had taken exactly the amount of time as it had to see off the Routemasters – two years and four months, and the choice of 9 December as the artics' last day was poetic justice if there ever was. And at more or less exactly the same time, LT 1, the first New Bus for London, or 'Borismaster', came off the production lines. One form of transport out, another form in, as had been the way of things probably since one pair of horses replaced another hauling one of George Shillibeer's early wooden conveyances.

This page: **Even if enthusiast and tourist opinion of these conveyances was universally negative, there was a small degree of fondness for them; drivers liked their general riding qualities and the increased degree of protection from the passengers, and general reliability was never an issue. To that end, the passage of EA 11040 was marked discreetly, with a small banner (left). The passenger load (standing, of course!) (middle) on the last journey and its driver (below) are also recorded for posterity.**
All: *Terry Wong Min*

Above: **The last bendy bus in London service was Hayes's EA 11040 (LK54 FKX), which departed White City at 00:05 for an 01:04 arrival at Hayes By-Pass. Some 'Last Day' Routemasters sported Union Jacks, which would not have done on these German-built buses!** *Bob Lear*

Network

First **7**

14th December 2011

Last London Bendies Convert to Double Deck
Media Spotlight Highlights A Great Team Effort

Last Friday saw the last day of bendy bus operation on Route 207 before they were converted to double deck operation for the run out on Saturday morning.

The conversion was carried out under close scrutiny from Transport for London and the Press, as it was the last bendy route in London to be converted, thus fulfilling the Mayor's manifesto pledge.

The team at Hayes delivered magnificently – thorough forward planning by Martin Moran and his team. Assistance from all departments and other depots ensured a smooth transition. It showed once again that we have the staff in place to deliver the big changes as well as excellent day to day operations.

A big thank you to everyone involved – drivers, controllers, engineers, trainers, admin and management – it was a great team result.

Well done.

Adrian Jones
Regional Managing Director
London & Berkshire

Photo by T WongMin

Please remove from Network notice Boards and recycle by 31st December 2011

Right: **Finally, the conversion of the 207 from EA to SN was accomplished to the satisfaction of management, as evinced in this First London press release.**

Friday 9 December 2011 was a cold day, which as much as anything deterred the last day of artics from being particularly well marked. The last eastbound bendy was EA 11049, but the final last journey on the 207 that day (spilling into Saturday) was the 00:05 leaving White City. This was operated by EA 11040, which carried about thirty passengers, most of which were enthusiasts – you'd have to be to want to travel to Hayes at one o'clock in the morning! There were no throngs of schoolchildren lining the pavements waving flags, but EA 11040 did find itself joined at Southall by a police escort, which shadowed it to Hayes By-Pass, where it terminated at 01:04. As they came out of service, the outgoing EAs were dispersed for storage between Hayes, Willesden Junction and the recently gained Acton premises. All of EAs 11039-11065 were returned to their lessors, Lombard Finance, by 30 December, while MALs 78 and 85 returned to Go-Ahead and the two acquired from elsewhere (EA 11000 and 11084) departed to Dawson Rentals on 31 January 2012. And that was the end of the artic in London service!

What passed for a requiem was in the expectedly triumphant proclamation by the Mayor that 'these bulky and ungainly monstrosities were always more suitable for the wide open vistas of a Scandinavian airport than for London's narrow streets

and I am glad to see the back of them.' In the same breath he made sure to extol the genuine environmental virtues of the 500 buses that had replaced them (including, by then, 200 hybrids), not to mention the perceived benefits of the upcoming New Bus for London and the £7m savings made from reducing fare evasion. Despite the admittedly expensive and premature turnover of vehicles on the twelve articulated-operated routes, all received peak-hour frequency boosts and an aggregate vehicle number increase of 141 buses, which in a city expanding as quickly as London would quickly be swallowed up and more needed.

Above: **A contemporary of the articulated bus in London and fading away at more or less the same time was the Saver ticket, introduced to help take the fare-accepting load off the driver but subsequently bettered by the Oyster card. Much was made of this mode of payment on bendy bus sides, exemplified by this reproduction of the second design of Saver ticket in the side window of one of First's EAs on its last day in service.** *Jack Marian*

Left: **And this is what replaced the EAs on the 207; the very last of the Polish Scanias, taken unusually by First and because they were the only organisation which could meet the specified delivery time. There were thirty-nine of them, exemplified by SN 36053 (YR61 RUA) at White City on 12 May 2012. Following First's momentous decision to pull out of London altogether, this bus passed to Metroline and is still plying the 207, but now under the identity of SN 1941.** *Author*

AFTER

Banished from service and from visibility, the surviving bendies could occasionally be sighted on non-PSV work; in the summer of 2012 Arriva's stored examples (most moving from Edmonton to Beddington Farm) were repainted all-red at Hants & Dorset for use on Olympic shuttles. This type of work was also performed by CT Plus, which leased four ex-Selkent examples from Dawson Rentals for the summer and all the way to 19 October. Go-Ahead's six MALs allocated to the Commercial Services department were transferred from Camberwell to Mandela Way in March while MALs 32-61 from the 436 remained in store at Belvedere (or later, for ten of them, Mandela Way) until February 2013, when they were returned to Lombard Leasing and sent on to store at Bruntingthorpe airfield. MALs 37 and 66 featured on Farnborough Air Show services in July 2012, while MAL 57 had received a white band by the end of 2012. Penny numbers of Arriva MAs drifted away during 2012, eight becoming works transport on a building site in County Kildare in the Irish Republic on behalf of Callinan Coaches in Galway, while five new to First London gravitated to McGill's and two to Uno. Early in 2013 MAs 27, 34 and 38 (ex-Arriva) were loaned to Isle of Man Transport, seven more soon joining them. The first three came back in March. Slow but continued disposals left just twenty in Arriva London North stock by July 2013, ten each at Edmonton and Derby, and the latter were shifted in August. The enforced closure of Edmonton on 1 March 2014 obliged the removal of the last nine MAs to storage at Coalville during January. And there they stay, gradually succumbing to the elements.

This page: **It's undeniable that for straightforward people movement, the artic has an edge, as long as most of them don't mind standing up or that they've got somewhere to look forward to going. A compromise is the park & ride concept, which at least allows those insistent on driving to make part of their journey by car. The cheerful colour combinations of the Bath Road operation operated by CT Plus with former London General artics is shown by, from top to bottom, MCAs 13 (BX02 YYS), 23 (BX02 YZG) and 17 (BX02 YZR), formerly MALs 11, 2 and 29.** All: *Steve Maskell*

Above: **In June 2012 McGill's of Greenock became the owners of five former Hayes EAs, one of which, D3613 (LK05 FCZ), is seen on Olympic Games work in this attractive livery. It was formerly known as EA 11060.**
Steve Maskell

Right: **Go-Ahead North East scooped up more than a few former London Central and General MALs for use in Gateshead. Resplendent in full gold X66 livery, 5348 (BP57 UYL) was ex-Mandela Way MAL 119. In March 2015 it moved to Brighton & Hove, becoming their 128.**
Steve Maskell

Right: **The blue and yellow livery of Dereham-based Konectbus sits nicely on everything, and the artics sent there by London General and London Central were no exception. This is 803 (BL57 OXM), formerly MAL 110. Until the full repaint could be carried out, the first order of business with Konectbus's artic acquisitions was to fit LED blinds.** *Steve Maskell*

Left: **Brighton & Hove's highly regarded operations took on artics without much trouble, using discarded London General and London Central examples from both batches thanks to the group tie-in under Go-Ahead. Most recently the company has seen fit to retire its 54-registered examples using cast-offs from Go-Ahead North East, and here at Old Steine on 15 May 2015 is 122 (BP57 UYG), formerly known as MAL 115 and intermediately Go-Ahead North East 5344.** *Author*

Left: **The story of the Citaro artics in Malta is arguably even more tragic than was their spell in London and deserves a 'warts and all' book of its own! For posterity, here at Cirkewwa during the summer of 2011 is an unidentified artic that has already had enough.**
Steve Morrey

Left: **At least the scenery in Malta is picturesque enough to make any kind of vehicle scrub up nicely, though the aquamarine livery of BUS 228 (formerly MA 111) jars against the prevailing architecture where the classic predecessors' deep yellow and orange had complemented it. This scene is at Bugibba on 3 July 2011.**
Richard Godfrey

Left: **The Citaro still has some say in the vehicle purchase policies of the big groups and their London subsidiaries, although the type has tended to fall in and out of fashion where British-bodied chassis have been deemed more suitable (not to mention cheaper). Thus the choice in 2012 by Stagecoach Selkent of fixed Citaros for the 227 (a route which would be eminently suited to articulated buses) to replace ageing Super Pointer Darts is unusual. While the deletion of buses' manufacturer badges was a quirk of the Olympics taking place at the same time this batch of twelve buses arrived, the Citaro looks just odd without its three-pointed star. This is Bromley's 23109 (LX12 DLE) departing Crystal Palace bus station on 4 August 2012.** *Author*

For all its effective surrender to the likelihood of fare evasion, the open-boarding format of the bendies was extended to Borismasters when it was reconfigured from a Routemaster-like concept to a three-doored vehicle, and this was rendered even more possible by the inevitable deletion of the customer assistant from subsequent conversions once the budget to pay such employees ran out. Criticism of both extremes in various media has been extensive and quite probably more so given the political aspect hung on the replacement of bendies by Borismasters. It wouldn't be at all surprising if a subsequent Labour GLA administration reintroduced them simply because their political opposition disliked them, and then the next Conservative administration after that reversed that policy, and so on and so on…

You almost feel sorry for the unhappy vehicles themselves. Aside from the well-documented fire issues (which have since been experienced by Tridents, another modern bus deliberately underpowered to fit into emissions legislation), there has been no slur on the Citaro design itself, which has progressed through two more seamless (yet familiar) iterations and continues to sell in large numbers, even to London in fixed format. Perhaps due to their sheer ease of replacement, comparatively few of 'our' bendies went on to further service, all the talk about how easily they could operate in cities outside London remaining just that, and the Malta adventure of the Arriva examples that went there proved to be an unmitigated disaster, for as unwittingly parallel reasons as in London.

Right: **We can't leave off this book without a cheap shot on the order of the 'Scandinavian airport' gag that associated Boris Johnson with the end of the bendies as lastingly as did Ken Livingstone's 'only dehumanised morons' crack. For that matter, there's no shame in airside transfer, which is just as legitimate an occupation for large box-like vehicles as stage carriage. And the livery is pretty too on National Express Stansted Airport's 13 (LX03 HDV), new as Stagecoach (both companies) 23030 and subsequently London Central MAL 120. On 20 July 2013 it has sprung a gearbox problem and is seen being taken away to Dawson Rentals. On an artic, no less!** *Graham Cooper*

Even so, strike me dead to say it, but there could yet be a place for this type of vehicle if carefully deployed: routes restricted physically to single-deckers but ever struggling with them, like the important 276 link across Stratford and Hackney or the 227 between Crystal Palace and Bromley North, plus unexpectedly useful local links that have outgrown their limited beginnings, like the W19.

The speculators among us might have selected second careers for the bendies within their existing companies (or groups, for the ambitious) so that they could live out the decade's lifespan that is that is all one can expect of modern buses. Within Arriva London North, routes like the 66, 173, 313, 444 and W15 would have seemed appropriate; if Arriva London South was to have been included, the 166, 289, 312 and T31, and if Arriva Kent Thameside were brought into play, the 126 and 286 would appreciate the extra capacity. Stagecoach's examples, meanwhile, could probably have made a favourable impression on any of routes 62, 178, 227, 296, 314, 396, 469, 499 and P4, while First's could have operated without undue difficulty on a choice of the 95, 187, 195, 224, 236, 487, A10, E7 and U1. Within the London Central and London General companies of Go-Ahead, routes 42, 108, 163, 164, 200, 219, 244, 355 and C10 could all have used larger-capacity buses than Darts, and if planning was extended to Metrobus, so could the 181, 284 and 358; Docklands Buses, the more recent of Go-Ahead's acquisitions in London, could have put them on any of the 167, 276, D6 or W19 to add seating capacity from the incumbent Darts or Dart-sized vehicles.

Where the future is concerned, tender specs for the Red Arrow routes in years to come could be most likely to at least entertain the idea of reintroducing bendies, since these were the routes made for them and on which they thrived. Then there are presently-minibus (or Dart-size-operated) routes whose road infrastructure can stand to be altered, like the W15; after all, considerable amounts of money were spent altering kerbs and bus-stop boxes to admit artics on their main-road trunk services and this infrastructure is all still in place. It's up to the London bus operators of the future, their corporate paymasters, and TfL controlling it all from on high, how far to go as to reconcile the needs of passengers of varying mobility with physical limitations of the capital's roads, the cultural and ergonomic expectations of regular passengers and tourists alike, and above all the financial ideals which, for good or ill, drive all transport-related decisions today.

Above: **Such a waste, even if one didn't like the things; all the fantasies of pulling the artics apart and fashioning fixed vehicles out of them came to nothing, and many of the Arriva MAs have simply fallen apart on site at the places they were trucked to. This fate fell to MA 92 (BX55 FUJ), new to Clapton and latterly of Edmonton but seen here with pieces missing at Beeston's during 2012.**
Wayne Bell

Left: **Plenty of life still left in these cast-offs, seen in March 2013 patiently waiting to be plucked from storage at Bruntingthorpe airfield. Just two examples are former First EA 11061 (LK05 FCM) and London General MAL 28 (BX02 YYR). Not all reclaimed bendies necessarily go back into service; most recently MA 30, late of Arriva, has joined an RML on one of those 'experiences' gifts; while slots to drive the Routemaster sold out more or less instantly, this hasn't been too unpopular.**
Dave Brundrit

APPENDICES

DELIVERIES AND ENTRY INTO SERVICE

DATE	FIRM	DELIVERIES	DATE	FIRM	INTO SERVICE (GAR)
05.02	*LG*	MAL 1-31			
			06.02	*LG*	MAL 1-31 (**RA**)
12.02	*LC*	MAL 34, 36, 38, 39			
	SEL	MA 1, 2			
01.03	*LC*	MAL 32, 33, 35, 37, 40-61			
	SS	23003, 23004			
02.03	*SS*	23005	02.03	*LC*	MAL 32-61 (**NX**)
03.03	*SS*	23006-23035	03.03	*SS*	23001-23035 (**PD**)
10.03	*FL*	ECA 3001, 3002, 3007, 3009, 3011, 3014, 3016, 3018, 3019			
11.03	*FL*	ECA 3003-3006, 3008, 3010, 3012, 3013, 3015, 3017, 3020-3032	11.03	*FL*	ECA 3031-3032 (**WJ**)
02.04	*ALN*	MA 2, 4, 11, 13			
03.04	*ALN*	MA 5-10, 12, 14-18, 22, 23, 25, 26, 28			
04.04	*ALN*	MA 1, 3, 19-21, 24, 27, 29	04.04	*ALN*	MA 1-29 (**EC**)
05.04	*ALN*	MA 30, 32, 33, 35			
	SEL	23037, 23041, 23043-23056			
	LC	MAL 36(ii)	05.04	*LC*	MAL 36(ii) (**NX**)
06.04	*ALN*	MA 31, 34, 36-39			
	SEL	23036, 3038-23040, 23042, 23057-23071, 23073-23077	06.04	*SEL*	23036-23071, 23073-23077 (**WA**)
	LC	MAL 51(ii)	06.04	*LC*	MAL 51(ii) (**NX**)
07.04	*ALN*	MA 41, 42, 50-56, 59-69, 72			
	SEL	23072	07.04	*SEL*	23072 (**WA**)
	LC	MAL 58(ii)	07.04	*LC*	MAL 58(ii) (**NX**)
08.04	*ALN*	MA 43-49, 57, 58, 70, 71, 73-76			
09.04	*LC*	MAL 78, 82			
			09.04	*ALN*	MA 30-39, 41-76 (**LV**)
10.04	*LC*	MAL 84, 85, 88			
			10.04	*ALN*	MA 40 (**LV**)
11.04	*LC*	MAL 62-77, 79-81, 83, 86, 87, 89-94	11.04	*LC*	MAL 62-94 (**Q**)
03.05	*FL*	EA 11039, 11040			
04.05	*FL*	EA 11041-11065	04.05	*FL*	EA 11039-11065 (**HS**)
07.05	*ALN*	MA 77, 79, 80, 85, 88			
08.05	*ALN*	MA 78, 81-84, 86, 87, 89-92, 94, 96, 101, 102			
09.05	*ALN*	MA 93, 95, 97-100, 103-124			
10.05	*ALN*	MA 125-130	10.05	*ALN*	MA 77-124 (**AE**)
11.05	*ALN*	MA 131-157			
12.05	*ALN*	MA 148			
			01.06	*ALN*	MA 125-157 (**EC**)
01.08	*LG*	MAL 101, 102, 104			
02.08	*LG*	MAL 95-100, 103, 105-119			
			03.08	*LG*	MAL 95-119 (**MW**)

ALN = Arriva London North   *EL* = East London Bus Group   *GAL* = Go-Ahead Group   *LC* = London Central
LG = London General   *FL* = First London   *SEL* = Stagecoach East London   *SS* = Stagecoach Selkent

RE-REGISTRATIONS

STAGECOACH EAST LONDON AND SELKENT

Date	Bus	Re-Registration
10.04	23076	LX04 LCV to WLT 886
11.04	23077	LX04 LCW to VLT 240
08.06	23063	LX04 LBZ to 630 DYE
11.07	23076	WLT 886 to LX04 LCV
07.11	23063	630 DYE to LX04 LBZ
07.11	23077	VLT 240 to LX04 LCW

ARRIVA LONDON NORTH

Date	Bus	Re-Registration
10.05	MA 5	BX04 MXB to 205 CLT
10.05	MA 85	BU05 VFD to 185 CLT
12.05	MA 17	BX04 MXR to 217 CLT
12.05	MA 19	BX04 MXT to 519 CLT
12.05	MA 30	BX04 MYY to 330 CLT
12.05	MA 61	BX04 NBL to 361 CLT
12.05	MA 70	BX04 NDE to 70 CLT
12.05	MA 80	BX05 UWZ to 480 CLT
12.05	MA 93	BX55 FUM to 593 CLT
12.05	MA 98	BX55 FUV to 398 CLT
12.05	MA 119	BX55 FVV to 319 CLT
12.05	MA 124	BX55 FWH to 124 CLT
01.06	MA 24	BX04 MXZ to 324 CLT
04.06	MA 124	124 CLT to BX55 FWH
05.09	MA 5	205 CLT to BX04 MXB
05.09	MA 17	217 CLT to BX04 MXR
05.09	MA 19	519 CLT to BX04 MXT
05.09	MA 24	324 CLT to BX04 MXZ
05.09	MA 30	330 CLT to BX04 MYY
06.09	MA 80	480 CLT to BX05 UWZ
12.09	MA 61	361 CLT to BX04 NBL
05.10	MA 85	185 CLT to BU05 VFD
05.10	MA 93	593 CLT to BX55 FUM
05.10	MA 98	398 CLT to BX55 FUV
05.10	MA 119	319 CLT to BX55 FVV
07.10	MA 70	70 CLT to BX04 NDE

RE-APPORTIONMENT AND RENUMBERING

Date	Transfer via Dawson Rentals	Buses with identity change
09.06	*Selkent* to *First London*	23001-23004 as EA 11066-11069
09.06	Demonstrator to *First London*	MD 1 as EA 11000
04.08	*Selkent* to *Arriva London North*	23005, 23006, 23008, 23012, 23015 as MA 161-165
05.08	*Selkent* to *Arriva London North*	23021 as MA 166
09.08	*Selkent* to *London Central*	23030 as MAL 120
09.08	*Selkent* to *First London*	23024 as EA 11084

DISPOSALS

Date	Firm	Buses
04.08	EL	23005-23008, 23012, 23014, 23015, 23018, 23020 to Dawson Rentals
05.08	EL	23009-23011, 23013, 23016, 23017, 23019, 23021-23026, 23029, 23030 to Dawson Rentals (23019 and 23029 re-acquired in February 2009)
04.09	ALN	MA 165 to Dawson Rentals (*not used*)
05.09	ALN	MA 161 to Dawson Rentals (*not used*)
10.09	LG	MAL 2-11, 13-31 to storage (disposal pool)
12.09	ALN	MA 9, 12, 40 to Arriva Merseyside
01.10	ALN	MA 162-164, 166 to Dawson Rentals
06.10	ALN	MA 10, 25 to Arriva Midlands
09.10	ALN	MA 5, 6, 13, 14, 19, 21, 23, 24, 32, 33, 41 to Arriva North West
10.10	FL	EA 11014, 11019 to Dawson Rentals
01.11	FL	EA 11002, 11006, 11012, 11022, 11028, 11031, 11069 to Dawson Rentals
02.11	ALN	MA 101, 123 to Arriva Malta
	FL	EA 11007, 11016 to Dawson Rentals
03.11	FL	EA 11004, 11008, 11015, 11020, 11027, 11029, 11032, 11067 to Dawson Rentals
04.11	ALN	MA 104, 105, 118, 119, 130, 134, 139, 149 to Arriva Malta
	FL	EA 11001, 11003, 11018, 11025 to Dawson Rentals
05.11	FL	EA 11010, 11011, 11013, 11017, 11021, 11023, 11066 to Dawson Rentals
	ALN	MA 54, 122 written off following fire damage
		MA 100, 102, 103, 113-115, 120, 121, 125, 138, 150, 151 to Arriva Malta
06.11	FL	EA 11005, 11009, 11024, 11026, 11030, 11068 to Dawson Rentals
	ALN	MA 82 written off following fire damage
		MA 106-110, 112, 116, 117, 124, 126-129, 131-133, 135-137, 140-143, 145-148, 152, 154 to Arriva Malta
07.11	SEL	23019, 23027-23029, 23031-23077 to Dawson Rentals
09.11	ALN	MA 2, 3, 8, 17, 28, 30, 35, 57, 67, 70 to store at Arriva Derby
		MA 36, 42, 46, 47, 51-53, 55, 56, 58, 61, 62, 72-74, 76, 77, 79, 88, 89 to store at Coalville
		MA 93 to Rossett's
		MA 155, 156 to Arriva Malta
	GAL	MAL 95, 96, 97 to Konect Bus
		MAL 98-107 to Brighton & Hove
		MAL 108, 109, 112-119 to Go North East
10.11	ALN	MA 93, 144, 157 to Arriva Malta
11.11	ALN	MA 4, 20, 60, 81, 83-87 to store at Coalville
		MA 50, 68, 90 to Arriva Malta
		MA 69 to Rossett's
	GAL	MAL 62-65 to Brighton & Hove
		MAL 67, 68, 70-75 to Go North East
		MAL 94 to Go South Coast
		MAL 92, 110, 111 to Konect Bus
12.11	ALN	MA 43 to TGM
	GAL	MAL 1, 12 to storage (disposal pool)
01.12	ALN	MA 48 to store at Coalville
		MA 91, 92, 94-99 to Arriva Malta (*formally from 24.04.12*)
	FL	EA 11000, 11084 to Dawson Rentals
	GAL	MAL 80, 88 to Konect Bus
		MAL 76, 77, 81, 83, 84, 86, 87, 90, 91, 93 to Go South Coast
06.12	ALN	MA 153 to store at Arriva Derby
08.12	ALN	MA 1 to Arriva North West
09.12	ALN	MA 62, 77, 81, 83, 87, 88 to Arriva Bus & Coach (dealership)
02.13	ALN	MA 26, 29 to Arriva Malta
	GAL	MAL 32-61 to Lombard Leasing
03.13	ALN	MA 22, 31, 60, 74, 78, 85, 86 to Arriva Malta
04.13	GAL	MAL 66 to unknown
05.13	ALN	MA 45 to Arriva North West
		MA 49, 59, 75 to Rossetts
		MA 7, 63, 69 to Arriva Malta
		MA 153 scrapped
07.13	ALN	MA 4, 20, 36, 37, 48, 55, 56, 58, 64, 65, 66, 70, 73, 80, 92 to North West Bus Sales
		MA 71 to Arriva Malta
08.13	ALN	MA 2, 3, 8, 17, 28, 30, 35, 57, 67, 72 to North West Bus Sales
10.13	GAL	MAL 69, 78, 79, 82, 85 to Ripley
12.13	ALN	MA 43 to TGM
02.14	ALN	MA 18 to Arriva Midlands

STATISTICS: THE ROUTES

Route Details

12	Dulwich–Oxford Circus (*Notting Hill Gate before bendies; section replaced by 390 extension*)
18	Euston–Sudbury
25	Oxford Circus–Ilford
29	Trafalgar Square–Wood Green (*Palmers Green before bendies; section replaced by 141 extension*)
38	Victoria–Clapton Pond
73	Victoria–Seven Sisters (*Tottenham before bendies*)
149	London Bridge Stn–Edmonton Green (*Ponders End before bendies; section replaced by new 349*)
207	Shepherd's Bush–Hayes By-Pass (*Uxbridge before bendies; section replaced by new 427*)
436	Paddington–Lewisham
453	Marylebone–Deptford
507	Victoria–Waterloo
521	Waterloo–London Bridge

Into Service

Route	Company	Buses	Date	Garage	PVR	(+/- previous)
507	LG	MAL 1-31	05.06.02	RA	9	(-1)
521	LG	MAL 1-31	05.06.02	RA	19	(+10)
436	LC	MAL 32-61	08.02.03	NX	26	(+8) including 36
453	SS	23001-23035	15.03.03*	PD	30	(+13) including 53
18	FL	ECA 3001-3032	15.11.03	WJ	27	(+1)
149	ALN	MA 1-28	24.04.04	SF	25	(-6)
25	SEL	23036-23077	26.06.04	MA	37	(-10)
73	ALN	MA 29-76	04.09.04	LV	41	(-14)
12	LC	MAL 62-94	06.11.04	Q	29	(-9)
207	FL	EA 11039-11065	09.04.05	HS	25	(-1) including 427
38	ALN	MA 77-134	29.10.05	AE	42	(-8)
29	ALN	MA 135-157	14.01.06	EC	29	(-2)

Contract Changes

Route	Company	Buses	Date	Garage	PVR	(+/-previous)
453	LG	MAL 95-119	16.02.08	MW	23	(+1)

Out of Service

Route	Company	Replacement Buses	Date	Garage	PVR	(+/-previous)
507	LG	MEC 1-50	25.07.09	RA	14	(+5)
521	LG	MEC 1-50	29.08.09	RA/MW	31	(+12)
38	ALN	DW 201-273, T 66-83	14.11.09	CT	70	(+28)
149	ALN	DW 298-336	16.10.10	LV	36	(+11)
18	FL	VN 37890-37942	13.11.10	WJ	48	(+16)
25	FC	VN 36101-36165	25.06.11	LI	59	(+15)
73	ALN	DW 428-464, HV 27-46	03.09.11	SF	51	(+8)
453	LG	E 163-202	24.09.11	MW	35	(+12)
12	LC	WVL 435-453, WHV 1-16	05.11.11	Q	41	(+10)
436	LC	E 208-228, EH 7-20	19.11.11	NX	32	(+6)
29	ALN	DW 465-498	26.11.11	WN	42	(+13)
207	FL	SN 36031-36065	10.12.11	HS	35	(+10)

STATISTICS: THE VEHICLES

First London AV 1-10
Volvo B7LA / Wright Eclipse Fusion AB56D,
hired 10.01-04.02 for route 207 (G) (new 03.01)

Fleet No	Registration	Chassis
AV 1	Y151 ROT	YV3R7C8151A000588
AV 2	Y152 ROT	YV3R7C8151A000589

(Bodies D423, D422)

Volvo B10LA / Wright Fusion ADP55D,
hired 10.01-04.02 for route 207 (G) (new 11-12.99)

Fleet No	Registration	Chassis
AV 6	V606 GGB	YV3R5A615XA001696
AV 7	V607 GGB	YV3R5A617XA001697
AV 8	V608 GGB	YV3R5A615XA001694
AV 10	V610 GGB	YV3R5A615XA001695

(Bodies B234, B235, B237, B238)

Go-Ahead London MAL 1-119
Mercedes-Benz Citaro O.530G AB49T
(MAL 95-119 AB47T)
(London General MAL 1-31, 95-119,
London Central MAL 62-94, inc. second 36, 51, 58)

Fleet No	Registration	Chassis
MAL 1	BX02 YZE	WEB62824323100892
MAL 2	BX02 YZG	WEB62824323100995
MAL 3	BX02 YZH	WEB62824323100996
MAL 4	BX02 YZJ	WEB62824323100997
MAL 5	BX02 YZK	WEB62824323100998
MAL 6	BX02 YZL	WEB62824323100999
MAL 7	BX02 YZM	WEB62824323101000
MAL 8	BX02 YZN	WEB62824323101001
MAL 9	BX02 YZO	WEB62824323101002
MAL 10	BX02 YZP	WEB62824323101003
MAL 11	BX02 YYS	WEB62824323101004
MAL 12	BX02 YYT	WEB62824323101005
MAL 13	BX02 YYU	WEB62824323101107
MAL 14	BX02 YYV	WEB62824323101108
MAL 15	BX02 YYZ	WEB62824323101110
MAL 16	BX02 YYW	WEB62824323101109
MAL 17	BX02 YZA	WEB62824323101111
MAL 18	BX02 YZB	WEB62824323101112
MAL 19	BX02 YZC	WEB62824323101113
MAL 20	BX02 YZD	WEB62824323101114
MAL 21	BX02 YYJ	WEB62824323101115
MAL 22	BX02 YYK	WEB62824323101116
MAL 23	BX02 YYL	WEB62824323101117
MAL 24	BX02 YYM	WEB62824323101118
MAL 25	BX02 YYN	WEB62824323101119
MAL 26	BX02 YYO	WEB62824323101120
MAL 27	BX02 YYP	WEB62824323101121
MAL 28	BX02 YYR	WEB62824323101122
MAL 29	BX02 YZR	WEB62824323101123
MAL 30	BX02 YZS	WEB62824323101124
MAL 31	BX02 YZT	WEB62824323101125
MAL 32	BN52 GWC	WEB62824323101886
MAL 33	BN52 GWD	WEB62824323102091
MAL 34	BN52 GWE	WEB62824323102122
MAL 35	BN52 GVU	WEB62824323102099
MAL 36	BD52 LNN	WEB62824323102258
MAL 36(ii)	BX04 NBD	WEB62824323104789
MAL 37	BD52 LNO	WEB62824323102147
MAL 38	BD52 LNP	WEB62824323102153
MAL 39	BD52 LNR	WEB62824323102158
MAL 40	BD52 LNT	WEB62824323102163
MAL 41	BD52 LNU	WEB62824323102173
MAL 42	BD52 LMU	WEB62824323102219
MAL 43	BD52 LMV	WEB62824323102223
MAL 44	BD52 LMX	WEB62824323102253
MAL 45	BD52 LMY	WEB62824323102120
MAL 46	BD52 LNA	WEB62824323102142
MAL 47	BD52 LNC	WEB62824323102179
MAL 48	BD52 LNE	WEB62824323102184
MAL 49	BD52 LNF	WEB62824323102199
MAL 50	BD52 LNG	WEB62824323102211
MAL 51	BD52 LNH	WEB62824323102228
MAL 51(ii)	BU04 EZK	WEB62824323105201
MAL 52	BD52 LMO	WEB62824323102246
MAL 53	BL52 ODK	WEB62824323102287
MAL 54	BL52 ODM	WEB62824323102300
MAL 55	BL52 ODN	WEB62824323102329
MAL 56	BL52 ODP	WEB62824323102333
MAL 57	BL52 ODR	WEB62824323102353
MAL 58	BL52 ODS	WEB62824323102357
MAL 58(ii)	BU04 UTM	WEB62824323105493
MAL 59	BL52 ODT	WEB62824323102367
MAL 60	BL52 ODU	WEB62824323102389
MAL 61	BL52 ODV	WEB62824323102390
MAL 62	BX54 EFC	WEB62824323105398
MAL 63	BX54 EFD	WEB62824323105402
MAL 64	BX54 UCM	WEB62824323105407
MAL 65	BX54 UCN	WEB62824323105408
MAL 66	BX54 UCO	WEB62824323105418
MAL 67	BX54 UCP	WEB62824323105419
MAL 68	BX54 UCR	WEB62824323105420
MAL 69	BX54 UCT	WEB62824323105421
MAL 70	BX54 UCU	WEB62824323105426
MAL 71	BX54 UCV	WEB62824323105433
MAL 72	BX54 UCW	WEB62824323105434
MAL 73	BX54 UCZ	WEB62824323105439
MAL 74	BX54 UDB	WEB62824323105447
MAL 75	BX54 UDD	WEB62824323105451
MAL 76	BX54 UDE	WEB62824323105452
MAL 77	BX54 UDG	WEB62824323105457
MAL 78	BX54 UDH	WEB62824323105463
MAL 79	BX54 UDJ	WEB62824323105470
MAL 80	BX54 UDK	WEB62824323105471
MAL 81	BX54 UDL	WEB62824323105474
MAL 82	BX54 UDM	WEB62824323105475
MAL 83	BX54 UDN	WEB62824323105476
MAL 84	BX54 UDO	WEB62824323105477
MAL 85	BX54 UDP	WEB62824323105478
MAL 86	BX54 UDT	WEB62824323105482
MAL 87	BX54 UDU	WEB62824323105483
MAL 88	BX54 UDV	WEB62824323105484
MAL 89	BX54 UDW	WEB62824323105485
MAL 90	BX54 UDY	WEB62824323105486
MAL 91	BX54 UDZ	WEB62824323105487
MAL 92	BX54 UEA	WEB62824323105489
MAL 93	BX54 UEB	WEB62824323105490
MAL 94	BX54 EFB	WEB62824323106490
MAL 95	BD57 WCY	WEB62828323114153
MAL 96	BD57 WCZ	WEB62828323114154
MAL 97	BD57 WDA	WEB62828323114155
MAL 98	BD57 WDC	WEB62828323114156
MAL 99	BD57 WDE	WEB62828323114157
MAL 100	BD57 WDK	WEB62828323114158
MAL 101	BD57 WDL	WEB62828323114159
MAL 102	BD57 WDM	WEB62828323114160
MAL 103	BD57 WDN	WEB62828323114161

MAL 104	BD57 WDP	WEB62828323114162
MAL 105	BD57 WDR	WEB62828323114163
MAL 106	BD57 WDS	WEB62828323114164
MAL 107	BD57 WDT	WEB62828323114165
MAL 108	BL57 OXJ	WEB62828323114166
MAL 109	BL57 OXK	WEB62828323114167
MAL 110	BL57 OXM	WEB62828323114168
MAL 111	BL57 OXN	WEB62828323114169
MAL 112	BL57 OXP	WEB62828323114170
MAL 113	BP57 UYE	WEB62828323114171
MAL 114	BP57 UYF	WEB62828323114172
MAL 115	BP57 UYG	WEB62828323114173
MAL 116	BP57 UYH	WEB62828323114174
MAL 117	BP57 UYJ	WEB62828323114175
MAL 118	BP57 UYK	WEB62828323114176
MAL 119	BP57 UYL	WEB62828323114177

Stagecoach London 23001-23077
Mercedes-Benz Citaro O.530G AB49T
(Selkent 23001-23035, East London 23036-23077)

Fleet No	Registration	Chassis
23001	LV52 VFW	WEB62824323101937
23002	LV52 VFX	WEB62824323102264
23003	LV52 VFY	WEB62824323102205
23004	LV52 VFZ	WEB62824323102271
23005	LV52 VGA	WEB62824323102278
23006	LX03 HCE	WEB62824323102516
23007	LX03 HCF	WEB62824323102525
23008	LX03 HCG	WEB62824323102533
23009	LX03 HCH	WEB62824323102544
23010	LX03 HCJ	WEB62824323102566
23011	LX03 HCK	WEB62824323102564
23012	LX03 HCL	WEB62824323102543
23013	LX03 HCN	WEB62824323102534
23014	LX03 HCP	WEB62824323102515
23015	LX03 HCU	WEB62824323102591
23016	LX03 HCV	WEB62824323102524
23017	LX03 HCY	WEB62824323102565
23018	LX03 HCZ	WEB62824323102567
23019	LX03 HDC	WEB62824323102577
23020	LX03 HDD	WEB62824323102583
23021	LX03 HDE	WEB62824323102584
23022	LX03 HDF	WEB62824323102585
23023	LX03 HDG	WEB62824323102590
23024	LX03 HDH	WEB62824323102591
23025	LX03 HDJ	WEB62824323102597
23026	LX03 HDK	WEB62824323102598
23027	LX03 HDL	WEB62824323102604
23028	LX03 HDN	WEB62824323102605
23029	LX03 HDU	WEB62824323102609
23030	LX03 HDV	WEB62824323102610
23031	LX03 HDY	WEB62824323102611
23032	LX03 HDZ	WEB62824323102616
23033	LX03 HEJ	WEB62824323102617
23034	LX03 HEU	WEB62824323102625
23035	LX03 HEV	WEB62824323102626
23036	LX04 KZG	WEB62824323105185
23037	LX04 KZJ	WEB62824323105186
23038	LX04 KZK	WEB62824323105187
23039	LX04 KZL	WEB62824323105191
23040	LX04 KZM	WEB62824323105192
23041	LX04 KZN	WEB62824323105193
23042	LX04 KZP	WEB62824323105198
23043	LX04 KZR	WEB62824323105199
23044	LX04 KZS	WEB62824323105200

23045	LX04 KZT	WEB62824323105204
23046	LX04 KZU	WEB62824323105205
23047	LX04 KZV	WEB62824323105210
23048	LX04 KZW	WEB62824323105211
23049	LX04 KZY	WEB62824323105218
23050	LX04 KZZ	WEB62824323105219
23051	LX04 LBA	WEB62824323105224
23052	LX04 LBE	WEB62824323105231
23053	LX04 LBF	WEB62824323105232
23054	LX04 LBG	WEB62824323105233
23055	LX04 LBJ	WEB62824323105238
23056	LX04 LBK	WEB62824323105239
23057	LX04 LBL	WEB62824323105246
23058	LX04 LBN	WEB62824323105247
23059	LX04 LBP	WEB62824323105252
23060	LX04 LBU	WEB62824323105253
23061	LX04 LBU	WEB62824323105254
23062	LX04 LBY	WEB62824323105259
23063	LX04 LBZ	WEB62824323105260
23064	LX04 LCA	WEB62824323105266
23065	LX04 LCC	WEB62824323105267
23066	LX04 LCE	WEB62824323105302
23067	LX04 LCF	WEB62824323105303
23068	LX04 LCG	WEB62824323105308
23069	LX04 LCJ	WEB62824323105309
23070	LX04 LCK	WEB62824323105319
23071	LX04 LCM	WEB62824323105320
23072	LX04 LCN	WEB62824323105325
23073	LX04 LCP	WEB62824323105326
23074	LX04 LCT	WEB62824323105383
23075	LX04 LCU	WEB62824323105384
23076	LX04 LCV	WEB62824323105389
23077	LX04 LCW	WEB62824323105397

First London ECA and EA
Mercedes-Benz Citaro O.530G AB49T
(ECA 3001-3032 later renumbered EA 11001-11032)

Fleet No	Registration	Chassis
ECA 3001	LK53 FAA	WEB62824324103624
ECA 3002	LK53 FAF	WEB62824324103810
ECA 3003	LK53 FAL	WEB62824324103811
ECA 3004	LK53 FAM	WEB62824324103815
ECA 3005	LK53 FAO	WEB62824324103816
ECA 3006	LK53 FAU	WEB62824324103829
ECA 3007	LK53 FBA	WEB62824324103835
ECA 3008	LK53 FBB	WEB62824324103840
ECA 3009	LK53 FBC	WEB62824324103841
ECA 3010	LK53 FBD	WEB62824324103851
ECA 3011	LK53 FBE	WEB62824324103852
ECA 3012	LK53 FBF	WEB62824324103853
ECA 3013	LK53 FBG	WEB62824324103860
ECA 3014	LK53 FBJ	WEB62824324103874
ECA 3015	LK53 FBL	WEB62824324103875
ECA 3016	LK53 FBN	WEB62824324103895
ECA 3017	LK53 FBO	WEB62824324103883
ECA 3018	LK53 FBU	WEB62824324103896
ECA 3019	LK53 FBV	WEB62824324103897
ECA 3020	LK53 FBX	WEB62824324103912
ECA 3021	LK53 FBY	WEB62824324103913
ECA 3022	LK53 FBZ	WEB62824324103922
ECA 3023	LK53 FCA	WEB62824324103929
ECA 3024	LK53 FCC	WEB62824324103930
ECA 3025	LK53 FCD	WEB62824324103939
ECA 3026	LK53 FCE	WEB62824324103949
ECA 3027	LK53 FCM	WEB62824324103950

ECA 3028	LK53 FCN	WEB62824324103951	MA 30	BX04 MYY	WEB62824323104797
ECA 3029	LK53 FCO	WEB62824324103957	MA 31	BX04 MZF	WEB62824323104812
ECA 3030	LK53 FCP	WEB62824324103965	MA 32	BX04 NDD	WEB62824323105146
ECA 3031	LK53 FCU	WEB62824324103967	MA 33	BX04 NDG	WEB62824323105153
ECA 3032	LK53 FCV	WEB62824324103989	MA 34	BX04 NDU	WEB62824323105169
EA 11039	LK54 FKX	WEB62824324105492	MA 35	BX04 NDV	WEB62824323105178
EA 11040	LK54 FKW	WEB62824324105509	MA 36	BX04 NDY	WEB62824323105179
EA 11041	LK05 FDC	WEB62824324105513	MA 37	BX04 NDZ	WEB62824323105180
EA 11042	LK05 FDD	WEB62824324105514	MA 38	BX04 NEF	WEB62824323105181
EA 11043	LK05 FDE	WEB62824324105516	MA 39	BX04 NEJ	WEB62824323105182
EA 11044	LK05 FDF	WEB62824324105524	MA 40	BX04 MYG	WEB62824323104712
EA 11045	LK05 FDJ	WEB62824324105605	MA 41	BX04 MYH	WEB62824323104762
EA 11046	LK05 FDG	WEB62824324105612	MA 42	BX04 MYJ	WEB62824323104766
EA 11047	LK05 FDL	WEB62824324105613	MA 43	BX04 MYK	WEB62824323104767
EA 11048	LK05 EZW	WEB62824324105618	MA 44	BX04 MYL	WEB62824323104772
EA 11049	LK05 EZX	WEB62824324105622	MA 45	BX04 MYM	WEB62824323104773
EA 11050	LK05 EZZ	WEB62824324105623	MA 46	BX04 MYN	WEB62824323104774
EA 11051	LK05 FCM	WEB62824324105628	MA 47	BX04 MYR	WEB62824323104780
EA 11052	LK05 FCN	WEB62824324105633	MA 48	BX04 MYS	WEB62824323104781
EA 11053	LK05 FCO	WEB62824324105636	MA 49	BX04 MYT	WEB62824323104787
EA 11054	LK05 FCP	WEB62824324105643	MA 50	BX04 MYU	WEB62824323104788
EA 11055	LK05 FCU	WEB62824324105650	MA 51	BX04 MYV	WEB62824323104795
EA 11056	LK05 FCV	WEB62824324105657	MA 52	BX04 MYW	WEB62824323104796
EA 11057	LK05 FBY	WEB62824324105665	MA 53	BX04 MYZ	WEB62824323104804
EA 11058	LK05 FCX	WEB62824324105672	MA 54	BX04 MZD	WEB62824323104805
EA 11059	LK05 FCY	WEB62824324105679	MA 55	BX04 MZE	WEB62824323104806
EA 11060	LK05 FCZ	WEB62824324105680	MA 56	BX04 MZG	WEB62824323104813
EA 11061	LK05 FDA	WEB62824324105684	MA 57	BX04 MZJ	WEB62824323104814
EA 11062	LK05 FBZ	WEB62824324105692	MA 58	BX04 MZL	WEB62824323104820
EA 11063	LK05 FCA	WEB62824324105701	MA 59	BX04 MZN	WEB62824323104821
EA 11064	LK05 FCD	WEB62824324105708	MA 60	BX04 NBK	WEB62824323104822
EA 11065	LK05 FCC	WEB62824324105715	MA 61	BX04 NBL	WEB62824323104827
			MA 62	BX04 NCF	WEB62824323104828
			MA 63	BX04 NCJ	WEB62824323104829

Arriva London North MA 1-157
Mercedes-Benz Citaro O.530G AB49T

Fleet No	Registration	Chassis	MA 64	BX04 NCN	WEB62824323104830
MA 1	BX04 MWW	WEB62824323104512	MA 65	BX04 NCU	WEB62824323105137
MA 2	BX04 MWY	WEB62824323104513	MA 66	BX04 NCV	WEB62824323105138
MA 3	BX04 MWZ	WEB62824323104542	MA 67	BX04 NCY	WEB62824323105139
MA 4	BX04 MXA	WEB62824323104552	MA 68	BX04 NCZ	WEB62824323105144
MA 5	BX04 MXB	WEB62824323104553	MA 69	BX04 NDC	WEB62824323105145
MA 6	BX04 MXC	WEB62824323104563	MA 70	BX04 NDE	WEB62824323105151
MA 7	BX04 MXD	WEB62824323104563	MA 71	BX04 NDF	WEB62824323105152
MA 8	BX04 MXE	WEB62824323104571	MA 72	BX04 NDJ	WEB62824323105159
MA 9	BX04 MXG	WEB62824323104581	MA 73	BX04 NDK	WEB62824323105160
MA 10	BX04 MXH	WEB62824323104582	MA 74	BX04 NDL	WEB62824323105161
MA 11	BX04 MXJ	WEB62824323104589	MA 75	BX04 NDN	WEB62824323105168
MA 12	BX04 MXK	WEB62824323104596	MA 76	BX04 NEN	WEB62824323105173
MA 13	BX04 MXL	WEB62824323104600	MA 77	BX05 UWV	WEB62824323107658
MA 14	BX04 MXM	WEB62824323104621	MA 78	BX05 UWW	WEB62824323107720
MA 15	BX04 MXN	WEB62824323104628	MA 79	BX05 UWY	WEB62824323107721
MA 16	BX04 MXP	WEB62824323104661	MA 80	BX05 UWZ	WEB62824323107722
MA 17	BX04 MXR	WEB62824323104662	MA 81	BU05 VFE	WEB62824323107723
MA 18	BX04 MXS	WEB62824323104663	MA 82	BU05 VFF	WEB62824323107724
MA 19	BX04 MXT	WEB62824323104674	MA 83	BX05 UXC	WEB62824323107725
MA 20	BX04 MXU	WEB62824323104690	MA 84	BU05 VFG	WEB62824323107726
MA 21	BX04 MXV	WEB62824323104691	MA 85	BU05 VFD	WEB62824323107727
MA 22	BX04 MXW	WEB62824323104692	MA 86	BU05 VFH	WEB62824323107728
MA 23	BX04 MXY	WEB62824323104703	MA 87	BU05 VFJ	WEB62824323107729
MA 24	BX04 MXZ	WEB62824323104720	MA 88	BX05 UXD	WEB62824323107730
MA 25	BX04 MYA	WEB62824323104726	MA 89	BX55 FWA	WEB62824323107731
MA 26	BX04 MYB	WEB62824323104734	MA 90	BX55 FWB	WEB62824323107732
MA 27	BX04 MYC	WEB62824323104740	MA 91	BX55 FUH	WEB62824323107733
MA 28	BX04 MYD	WEB62824323104754	MA 92	BX55 FUJ	WEB62824323107734
MA 29	BX04 MYF	WEB62824323104761	MA 93	BX55 FUM	WEB62824323107735
			MA 94	BX55 FUO	WEB62824323107736
			MA 95	BX55 FUP	WEB62824323107737